RIVER & COASTAL WALKS IN SUFFOLK
Volume One

Mel Birch

a
CASTELL
publication

RICHARD CASTELL PUBLISHING LIMITED

RIVER & COASTAL WALKS IN SUFFOLK - VOLUME ONE
COPYRIGHT © 1997 RICHARD CASTELL PUBLISHING LIMITED

Text © 1997 Mel Birch

Front Cover:
River Gipping near Needham Market (Gary Birch)

ISBN 0 948134 42 9

First Published May 1997 by
RICHARD CASTELL PUBLISHING LIMITED
Thwaite, Eye, Suffolk IP23 7EE.

Printed by
THE GIPPING PRESS
Lion Barn Industrial Estate, Needham Market, Suffolk IP6 8NZ

CONTENTS

The River Orwell

INTRODUCTION

IF YOU HAVE yet to be introduced to the delights of Suffolk's beautiful river network and Heritage Coast, you will find exploring the walks in the two volumes of this book, and discovering those secret places only accessable to those on foot, a memorable and enduring experience.

Bordered on two sides by rivers and on a third by the North Sea coast, and with two other major rivers running through it, few counties contain such a variety of river scenery or abundance of wildlife, flora and fauna, most of which is now thankfully protected.

The **Orwell** is now unquestionably the most important waterway, providing a link between the county town and major port of Ipswich and the Continent. Yet despite this commercial activity, it remains one of the most beautiful.

The **Stour** is really two rivers in one. Its early course passes through the beautiful Dedham Vale on the Essex and Suffolk borders - where it has been immortalised in the paintings of John Constable, but having freed itself at Manningtree, and with its own Continental Ferry port of Harwich in sight, it throws back its banks and becomes the county's largest river, a mile wide in places, twice that of the Orwell.

The eerie marshes and mudflats bordering the **Deben** evoke the perfect atmosphere for a river steeped in history; the whole antiquity of Suffolk has its roots here. Traces of the ancient East Anglian Kingdom of the Wuffingas lie scattered along its banks while the world-famous Sutton Hoo Treasure Ship was dragged from its shores to a ritual burial overlooking the water opposite Woodbridge.

The **Waveney** forms the border with Norfolk, its tranquil course passing through those scenes of woodland, pasture and water-meadow readily associated with the county. Yet it has its moments; at Oulton it becomes a part of the Broads and takes holiday cruisers on into Norfolk.

Of those playing a lesser but still vital role in the county's heritage, the **Gipping** is no doubt proud of having given birth to the Orwell. It provided a vital trade link carrying goods between the mid-Suffolk town of Stowmarket and Ipswich from where it continues to the sea as the tidal Orwell.

The **Blyth**, itself once a busy trading route, now forms a pleasant backwater running through pastural water meadows. Standing high above its banks is one of Suffolk's most memorable sights, that of Blythburgh Church.

The calm waters of the **Ore** and **Butley** rivers were mainly created by the shingle spit which destroyed the port of Orford.

The **Alde**, on whose banks stands the world-famous concert hall at Snape Maltings, has given inspiration to poets and composers, while the **Lark**

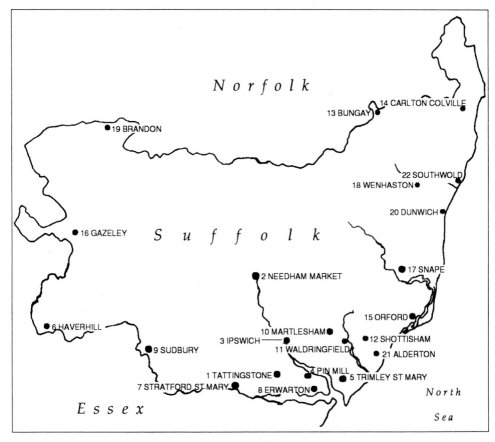

MAP OF SUFFOLK SHOWING STARTING POINTS

keeps memories of a terrible carnage in its waters one fateful day in 1173 near Bury St Edmunds.

Along the 45 miles of **Heritage Coast**, stretching from Corton in the north to Felixstowe in the south, the North Sea has held the destiny of every town and village, treating all with faint regard to wealth and favour. While today the port of Felixstowe plays an ever-increasing role in world trade, during medieval times, before the town itself even existed, this role had been played by others with equal fervour. Their names seem so unlikely today, yet Walberswick, Blythburgh, Dunwich, Orford, Covehithe and others were all influencial trading ports. They had flourishing fishing industries, and built ships and sailed them to fight for king and country. Their greatest battle however, was with the sea on which they depended; as we shall see, in every case this was a battle they were to lose.

As the North Sea remapped the coastline Dunwich, at one time a city and the most important port on the east coast, was lost beneath the waves and a large part of Aldeburgh was washed away to be dumped unceremoniously as a shingle spit farther along the coast at Orford, cutting off that busy port from the sea and leaving its great castle as a lone reminder of former glory.

Others turn different faces to the elements. Southwold, prim and neat, hides its fear of further losses with an almost arrogant air, but at stark and windswept Shingle Street, neither the continual conflict with the sea nor the sense of complete abandonment is as easily disguised.

Such a wealth of history and mood, such a stock of melancholy memories. I hope, like me, you will experience them all during the course of these first twenty-two walks.

As always, please remember to:

FOLLOW THE COUNTRY CODE

Leave livestock, and crops and machinery alone.

Take your litter home.

Help to keep all water clean.

Protect wildlife, plants and trees.

Take special care on country roads.

Make no unnecessary noise.

Enjoy the countryside and respect its life and work.

Guard against all risk of fire.

Fasten all gates.

Keep your dogs under close control.

Keep to public paths across farmland.

Use gates and stiles to cross fences, hedges and walls.

ALTON WATER
Walk 1: Stutton & Tattingstone

Start: *Take the A137 south from Ipswich and fork left to Tattingstone White Horse. Continue towards Tattingstone itself and park in the small car park on the far side of Lemons Hill Bridge.*

O.S.Maps: *Landranger 169; Pathfinder 1053.*

Distance: *2½, 7 or 9 miles.*

Refreshments: *Tattingstone White Horse pub.*

Description: *It would be difficult to get lost on this walk which traces the boundary of the reservoir. Although the western bank is level and easy going, the eastern side is surprisingly hilly and a little frustrating as your progress is delayed by the various excursions inland to follow the numerous inlets.*

Alton Water is Anglian Water's 2000 million gallon reservoir providing the main source of water for much of Ipswich and the southern part of Suffolk from Stowmarket to Felixstowe. Constructed between 1974-6, it covers 390 acres and was officially opened in 1987 by The Princess Royal.

Although its creation, which necessitated the flooding of the delightful Tattingstone valley and the loss of several properties, caused much heated debate at the time, the reservoir can now offer excellent recreational and leisure facilities to the many thousands who visit each year.

In 1992 these facilities were greatly improved with an extension to the Water Sports Centre and the completion of a purpose-built Visitors' Centre. A new cycle track skirts the reservoir, some of it on special track, offering a picturesque 10 mile circuit; cycles can be hired throughout the year.

Among the wide range of birds you can expect to see on your walk are herons, skylarks, snipe, crested grebe, coots and bullfinches. Some 40,000 trees have been planted around Alton and two nature reserves give quiet shelter and peace to a whole variety of wildlife.

FOR THE 7 MILE WALK come out of the car park and walk across Lemons Hill Bridge to join the description at point *.

FOR THE SHORT 2½ MILE OR FULL 9 MILE WALK go through the gate at the back of the car park to pick up a well-used path which heads through the trees.

At the end of the trees go over the stile ahead and turn right to head up the right side of a cultivated field. Pick up a dirt track and then join a metalled track which runs to Cragpit Farm over on your right. You turn left and head away from the farm towards the main A137.

Do not join it but instead turn right heading down a now abandoned metalled lane.

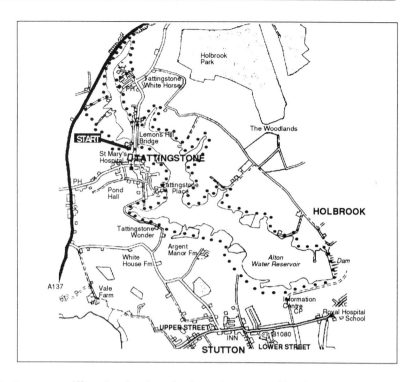

At the bottom you will notice that it ends abruptly - severed by the creation of the reservoir - to appear again on the far side. Turn left and follow the path which goes through an area of grassland. At the fence and a stile into the cultivated field between yourself and the main road, turn right without negotiating it and, keeping the fence on your left, continue on a grassy path which meets the main road at the point where it bridges the end of the reservoir.

Carry on along a wide grassy strip well back from the busy road. On the far side of the bridge go over a stile on your right and follow the path almost back on yourself down into scrub beside Alton Water, here often little more than a marsh. From here as you follow the bank of the reservoir you often have an alternative route. The main firm track which also caters for cyclists is set back and generally runs along the higher ground with some short but steep climbs. The narrow grassy path which is more level, winds its way along the bank regularly returning to the main track.

You eventually arrive at Lemons Hill Bridge *. To complete your short walk just cross the bridge back to the southern car park.

The 7 mile and full walk continue by crossing the road and walking through the northern car park. Beyond, follow the well-walked path as it heads inland skirting

9

an inlet. You may not need to follow this inlet to its end, as it may be possible to cross the marshy ground at a dry place and head back on the far side. This will happen on several occasions along this eastern side. On the far side is the impressive pile of Tattingstone Place, followed by Tattingstone Wonder. Pass Crag Hall Covert and two further inlets, then the draw-off tower before finally arriving at the dam, an impressive piece of engineering holding back 2000 million gallons of water from the remaining unflooded section of the Tattingstone valley. Walk over the large expanse of neatly mown grass and take the path over the dam. On the far side turn right and head across the grass to pass to the left of the collection of moored boats slowly converging on the metalled drive to your left. You arrive at the Visitors' Centre where there is information, toilets and possibly some light refreshments.

Carry straight on picking up the cycle track which follows the boundary fence, though you are free to roam over the grassy banks to the water. Later beyond the mown area you can take grassy paths which lead you down beside the lake and back to the main path in an arc. Pass through the delightful Larch Wood and soon arrive at a gate by a country road. Opposite is what first appears to be a flint church.

> Tattingstone Wonder is, in fact, not a church at all but a group of three cottages built as homes for his workmen by Edward White who required a church view for his home at nearby Tattingstone Place. He is reported as saying that as people wondered at nothing he would give them something to wonder at. Closer inspection shows it to be a folly with a mock tower.

Do not enter the road but cross the lane and continue along the track running parallel with the road. This sweeps round the inlet of water and climbs beside the road. At a point just before the road bends left into Tattingstone village, go off right and pick up a short length of narrow metalled lane. This ends abruptly, cut off by the reservoir and you turn left along a track. (On the far side of the water the lane recommences at the point you were walking earlier).

The track arrives at Tattingstone Place and you skirt the garden boundary wall.

> Tattingstone Place was built by Edward White around 1750 on the moated site of an earlier house.

Eventually you arrive back at Lemons Hill Bridge and cross the road back to the car park and your starting point.

The River Gipping

. . . *What tho' thy neighbour Orwell boats*
His variegated length of coast,
His busy trade and shipping;
Tell him that happiness may stray
Where pomp could never find the way,
And glide thro' vales with Gipping.

No envious sands thy course perplex,
No howling storms thy waters vex,
Their shores of Verdure stripping;
Thy peaceful streams translucent glide,
While Flow'rets bend on either side
To view themselves in Gipping . . .

(Elizabeth Cobbold)

Sproughton Mill (Walk 3)

THE RIVER GIPPING
Walk 2: Needham Market & The Creetings

Start:	*Park in the small car park in Barrett's Lane off the northern end of Needham Market High Street by Barclays Bank. There are toilets here.*
O.S.Maps:	*Landranger 155; Pathfinder 1007.*
Distance:	*8 miles.*
Refreshments:	*There are no refreshments on the walk but there are adequate pubs and tea shops in Needham Market itself.*
Description:	*The first half of the walk is mainly along firm tracks with one section of field walking; you will also have to cross and negotiate the steep banks either side of the A14 dual-carriageway. The remainder of the walk is beside the river.*

COME OUT ON THE HIGH STREET and turn left and right down Hawks Mill Lane. Pass under the railway bridge and go over the humpback bridge passing the converted mill. Go over the second road bridge bearing left and half way towards the bend along St Mary's Road turn off right along a well-worn footpath between open fields.

The path bears left and then goes right and left through an opening in the hedge passing an Anglian Water pumping station. Immediately fork right over rough ground heading to the right of cottages. Cross straight over the metalled country lane up a sunken bridleway between hedges. At the top go up the bank above the busy A14.

Turn right and walk a few yards until you are level with a break in the crash barriers below. Carefully clamber down the bank and cross the dual-carriageway here, making a good allowance for the speed of the traffic. Climb the bank beyond to the stile and footpath sign. Head up the meadow beside the post and rail fence towards houses. At the end of the fence a distinct grassy track leads you straight ahead and out into a country lane. Turn right and immediately fork left and right to take the signposted track passing to the left of 'Fourwinds'. (Do not continue along the metalled lane passing to the right of the bungalow which is also signposted as a footpath).

You are now on Sally Woods Lane, a wide firm track heading away between cultivated fields. As the traffic noise from the A14 receedes you have lovely open views across undulating countryside. At a point where the field on your left ends, the track suddenly bends sharp right and you leave it by turning off left to follow the edge of the field on your left along a narrow path which later opens out into a farm track, at first rough, but later firm.

You eventually arrive at a T-junction of ways. The track crossing is Holts Lane which a short distance to the right joins the notorious A140 Ipswich to Norwich road, but thankfully you turn left. When the well-worn farm track bends right

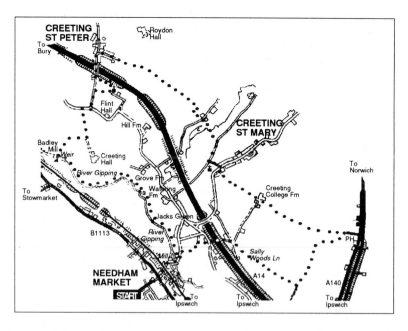

you continue straight on along what is now a green lane running between high hedges and trees, and later as a wide grassy track between open fields. There are fine views over the Gipping Valley.

You reach Creeting College Farm staying left of the buildings and going right on a concrete farm drive prior to the farm house as instructed by the footpath sign. Go left over the concrete farmyard heading for the left-hand exit where you pass to the right of the flint garden wall. Now head away from the farm down a dirt track between open fields.

Continue beside the fenced gardens of a small development of modern houses to reach the road at Creeting St Mary. Your route is right and left down the steep hill but you may first wish to visit the church opposite.

> St Mary's Church is one of two which stood in this churchyard, and the only one remaining of three which once represented three separate parishes, St Mary, All Saints and St Olave. The parishes were consolidated under Creeting St Mary in 1884. All Saints Church had been taken down in 1813 and St Olave's was disused as far back as 1660. St Mary's is of mainly 13th and 14th century date with traces of Norman work in the south door. Lost completely are the two Benedictine priories which once stood in the St Mary and St Olave parishes. The more important of the two was St Mary's Priory founded in 1156.

14

At the junction at the bottom of the hill turn right and walk along the metalled lane to a point where the field on your left ends. Here turn left along a path enclosed by high hedges. Pass through an area of fen, scrub and light woodland - usually damp in places - and go over a footbridge.

> The Fen is an area of Sedge and Osier beds. The sedge was used as ridging on thatched roofs and for animal litter and the osiers for baskets and general weaving.

Continue along a faint path, go right over a plank bridge and left to pass between the thatched Fen House Farm and its detached garage block and on up the drive to join Fen Lane.

Go left for a few yards before turning right to walk up the right side of a cultivated field. Follow the garden boundary and, when it ends, keep straight on in the same direction up the open field to a point where the right hand field boundary turns left and right. Turn right at this point and cross the field to join this field boundary. Now carry on as before up the field. When you reach the corner cross the ditch by a plank bridge and cross diagonally over to the left side of the next field - cutting off the corner - and carry on as before. Follow the field boundary left, and half way to the field corner, a footpath sign sends you right to continue straight up over the open field. A considerable consolation for the difficulty of the route on this section of the walk is the wonderful views; you can literally see for miles.

Reach the end of the hedge line and carry on along the right side of the field with the hedge on your right. You head down to a small pumping station where sanity returns and you can join a wide farm track following the left side of the next field. At the end of the field do not turn right as directed by the footpath sign in front of the houses, but carry straight on to join the end of a lane with properties on either side.

Come out on the road in the village of Creeting St Peter and turn left. Just over the A14 flyover you have the chance of a short detour to visit the church (although it was locked on my visit). If you wish to pass, carry on down Pound Road to the junction.

To visit the church take the footpath sign left to walk along the top of the embankment beside a cultivated field on a metalled path. At the end of the field an earthen path goes right to the church.

> The north door of St Peter's Church is Norman but the bulk of the church is Decorated. On the north wall are the remains of a magnificent painting of St Christopher with a scroll inscribed in Latin 'Whosoever looks at the picture of St Christopher shall assuredly on that day be burdened with no weariness.'

Leave by the metal gate through the churchyard opposite the porch. Turn right on

15

a track and carry on heading along the right side of a field. At the end negotiate concrete steps down to Pound Road where you turn left and continue to the junction. Turn right towards Stowmarket, and after about 120 paces arrive at the white gates and drive leading to Creeting Hall. Turn left. Half way to the hall turn off right and walk along a rough track between open fields. Just past a pond on your right the track bends left and right gradually descending into the Gipping Valley. At the end of the field go over a footbridge and stile into a meadow. Cross straight over and negotiate a fence to arrive at the River Gipping by a bridge. Just to your right is Badley Mill. Turn left and negotiate stiles to proceed along the left bank back to Needham Market.

> The river and gravel pits along the Gipping Valley provide an attraction for birdlife - kingfishers, canada geese, coots, mallard, grebe and the occasional heron and cormorant can be seen. The water margins offer a refuge for water voles and coypu as well as flag iris, purple loosestrife, marsh woundwort and many varieties of rushes, reeds and sedges. The river supports several species of freshwater fish including roach, bream and pike. Many of the meadows through which the river meanders have been ploughed up or changed to pasture but those that remain support a wide variety of plant life - ragged robin, ladies smock, fleabane, marsh orchid and many others. Another feature of the valley are the trees and hedgerows which add interest to the landscape. Particularly noticeable from the river path are the alders which grow out from the river bank, the once pollarded willows and the occasional black poplar.
>
> The history of navigation on the Gipping will be told on the next walk.

You eventually pass rather spectacular lock gates dropping the river several feet and arrive back at the road bridge. Climb the steps and carefully join the road turning right to recross the bridge and return to Needham Market street and your starting point.

THE RIVER GIPPING
Walk 3: Ipswich to Sproughton

Start: From Ipswich railway station drive along Ranelagh Road and turn left at the traffic lights into Ancaster Road. Go under the railway bridge and, where the road bends right carry straight on and park just along the unmade road.

O.S.Maps: Landranger 169; Pathfinder 1030.

Distance: 6½ miles.

Refreshments: Wild Man pub at Sproughton.

Description: The walk is divided into three sections. The first involves leaving the confines of Ipswich itself via a pleasant walk through Gippeswyk, one of the town's many fine parks, and a walk along the busy London Road with a brief visit to Chantry park and Chantry House. The second takes us along country paths to the village of Sproughton, and the final section leads us back to town along the Gipping tow path.

WALK BACK DOWN Ancaster Road and turn left through the entrance gates of Gippeswyk Park. Set off along the path running parallel with the railway along the right side of the park past football pitches which, in season, may provide additional entertainment. At the end, continue ahead to reach the busy London Road where you cross the road with care and turn left.

After about half a mile turn right through the entrance gates of Chantry Park almost opposite to the entrance to Chantry Estate. Walk down the tree-lined metalled drive. Turn left after the last football pitch on the left and pass in front of Chantry House, now a convalescent home under the Sue Ryder Foundation.

The Chantry, standing in extensive parkland which covers 124 acres, was given to the town in 1927 by Sir Arthur Churchman as a public park. The mansion was built in the early 18th century by Edward Ventris and later became the seat of the Kelly family.

The gravel path goes right and left to pass through the rose garden and then bears right to pass down the side of the house. At the front of the house turn to head away down the metalled drive leading out of the park, passing a row of magnificent old trees.

Out on the Hadleigh Road, cross over and turn left. Walk along the footpath to a point on the bend in the road immediately past the new high brick wall of Chantry Grove, now called Manderley Manor, where you locate a narrow well-worn path enclosed by high hedges and trees. On your right is a wall, then a high wire fence. Cross a stile, after which the path continues, a little precariously, along the top of a bank. Go over two further stiles either side of a grazing meadow entrance, often muddy, and then along the side of a cultivated field. Pass to the right of cottages to reach a country lane.

Turn right and walk to the end where you locate an underpass to cross the busy A14 trunk road. Beyond, pick up Church Lane and head into Sproughton to reach the church. Enter the churchyard.

> All Saints Church is mostly 14th and 15th century with a hammer-beam roof. There are many memorials including one of 1634 to Elizabeth Bull.

Leave the churchyard by a single wooden gate to the road. Opposite is Sproughton Mill. Your route is right to cross the River Gipping by the road bridge, but if you first require a refreshment stop turn left instead and walk to the top of the street to visit the Wild Man which offers anything from a drink and snack to a full meal.

> The four storey red-brick mill at Sproughton in its picturesque situation opposite the church has been restored and converted into other uses. Although there used to be four pairs of stones, none of the machinery has survived.

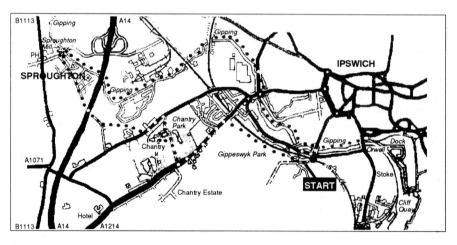

Back on the route, after crossing the bridge turn immediately right down the steps to the river bank where you commence your walk back to Ipswich.

> The River Gipping was used as a navigable waterway as far back as the 12th and 13th centuries when much of the stone used to build the Abbey at Bury St Edmunds was brought up river to Rattlesden, while in the 17th century church bells were carried from Ipswich to Stowmarket.

In 1790, a Parliamentary Act was passed to construct a 17 mile canal from Ipswich Docks to Stowmarket and 200 men began work in the same year to widen and deepen the channel. Fifteen locks were constructed to enable barges up to 13 ft. wide and 60 ft. long, with a draught of 3 ft. to carry up to 30 tons of cargo between the two centres.

When the canal opened in 1793 under the Gipping Navigation Company it took a horse-drawn barge 10 hours to travel upstream and 7 hours to return. In its heyday up to 30 barges were using the Gipping to transport cargoes such as coal, slate, timber, lime, manure, chemicals and gun cotton. In 1846 the railways arrived and the canal company leased out the canal to the railway company for a period of 42 years. Not surprisingly tolls were raised and the waterway neglected encouraging traffic to transfer to the railway. Stowmarket was last reached by barge in the early 1900s.

You negotiate a major pumping station, then, as you approach the sugar beet factory, the path is cindered.

At the first railway bridge and automatic flood barrier you have to negotiate some concrete steps before continuing on ahead. The river begins to widen and industrial sites nudge the perimeter fence. Pass under Yarmouth Road and by the Suffolk Retail Park on your left. Immediately after this the path is interrupted by the road bridge and you need to climb the steps on your left.

Cross the busy London Road with care and turn right. At the end of the bridge go down the steps on your left and continue along the right bank of an overgrown spur of the Gipping.

At the time of my visit work was being carried out on the next bridge and I was taken on a diversion over the bridge and past the recycling plant before crossing the busy West End Road. Then turning left to go down to the river and pick up the path again. Hopefully this disruption will have ended by the time of your walk. Go under another railway bridge carrying a goods spur to the industrial area. The path bears left and you see the Princes Street Bridge and the railway station ahead. You can leave the path here by climbing the steps to Princes Street.

If you have the time and energy you may wish to continue on the path for the short return walk to Stoke Bridge.

Stoke Bridge is a significant point on the Gipping's journey to the sea, for it is from this point that the river becomes tidal and changes its name to Orwell. There was a bridge recorded at Stoke as far back as 970. From here you can view the Old Customs House built in 1844 and the Wet Dock, constructed in 1841 - at that time the largest enclosed dock in England.

Return to Princes Street and walk the short distance to the junction in front of the station. Turn right and then go left into Ancaster Road, under the railway bridge and back to your starting point.

19

Woolverstone Marina (Walk 4)

The River Orwell

Orwell, delightful stream, whose waters flow
Fring'd with luxuriant beauty to the main!
Amid thy woodlands taught, the Muse could fain,
On thee, her grateful eulogy bestow.
Smooth and majestic though thy current glide,
And bustling commerce plough thy liquid plain;
Tho' grac'd with loveliness thy verdant side,
While all around enchantment seems to reign.

(I.I.Shewell)

FORMED at a point near Stoke Bridge in Ipswich where the river Gipping, flowing from Stowmarket, meets the sea waters and becomes tidal.

Ipswich, the chief settlement on the river, trailed Dunwich in 1279 when it had thirty great ships to the latter's eighty, but with Dunwich's decline in the Middle Ages the town built up a sizeable fleet. Its facilities were such that in the 14th century Edward III and the Black Prince fitted out 500 ships here for the Calais expedition.

Apart from giving access to world trade and shipbuilding, the Orwell provided the town with another lucrative industry during the 19th century, coprolite. This fossilised animal dung was dug up in great quantities all along the Orwell-Deben peninsula and ground down to form a fertiliser. By 1877, ten thousand tons were being shipped each year. The industry is remembered in Coprolite Street in Ipswich.

Smuggling was always prevalent along such a trade conscious river and apart from the white cat of Woolverstone (see Walk 4), Pin Mill, Levington and the other little picturesque quays along the banks all have their stories to tell.

At one time ships could not reach the town of Ipswich itself and had to lay anchor in Butterman Bay from where their cargo was moved by barge. Later the central channel was dredged allowing even the largest ships to make the port; the annual Pin Mill Barge Race commemorates those days.

Ipswich has always been in the forefront of British port development. When constructed in 1842, its wet dock was the largest in the country.

Felixstowe, only a small village in the middle of the last century, has taken over the mantle as chief rival to Ipswich, and its position at the head of the estuary has given it a positive advantage in trade with the Continent. It now proudly boasts its hard won title as Britain's largest and most successful container port.

THE RIVER ORWELL
Walk 4: Pin Mill, Woolverstone & Chelmondiston

Start:	*Take the B1456 south from Ipswich passing under the Orwell Bridge. At the end of Chelmondiston street turn left down to Pin Mill and park in the public car park on the left.*
O.S.Maps:	*Landranger 169; Pathfinder 1053 & 1054.*
Distance:	*5 miles.*
Refreshments:	*The Butt & Oyster at Pin Mill. Pubs off the route in Chelmondiston.*
Description:	*The walk is easy and a complete delight especially the sections along the Orwell itself, much of which is through areas of beautiful woodland - some under The National Trust - and elevated above the river with superb views.*

LEAVE THE CAR PARK and turn left to walk down the lane to meet the river by the Butt & Oyster.

Pin Mill, a designated Conservation Area, probably grew up as a station for pilot boats, close to the dangerous mud banks above Downham Reach. The 17th century Butt & Oyster inn, delightfully situated right on the river's edge, has connections with smuggling and the books of Arthur Ransome. The Orwell laps against its walls and from its windows you will often look out on Thames barges moored in the river, surviving examples of once important coastal trading vessels, many of which were locally built. Larger sailing ships would unload their cargoes into the barges for local distribution. An annual race takes place when barges sail down the Orwell from Butterman's Bay east of Pin Mill.

Turn left to proceed along the foreshore stepping over the river Grindle, here just a trickle. Just beyond the boatyard fork left (do not turn sharp left under the arch) walk along a shingle drive between two properties and then bear right to pick up a well-used footpath leading you into open countryside.
Beyond the stile take the right fork across a cultivated field. Beyond, on the edge of woodland, the path divides again and you turn right into the wood. There now commences a superb section of walking on the edge of Woolverstone Park, lightly wooded, interspersed with fine mature oaks, and with the Orwell on your right.

The River Orwell, commencing at Stoke Bridge in Ipswich, the point at which the Gipping becomes tidal, is not only popular for yachting but an important commercial channel carrying international cargo and containers between Ipswich Docks and the Continent. Its estuary is often considered to be the most ornithologically diverse in Suffolk. Eleven species of wildfowl and waders can reach numbers of national importance. Wildfowl particularly evident here include coot, mallard, sheldrake and wigeon but sightings can often be made of pintail, shoveler and, in severe winters, scaup. The river is of international importance for redshank, while other more common waders include dunlin, knot, oystercatcher and turnstone.

Eventually you reluctantly emerge at Woolverstone Marina. As you pass in front of the modern club house of the Royal Harwich Yacht Club you can see the Orwell Bridge in the distance ahead. When your footpath meets a concrete road turn left by Cat House.

The curious Cat House, a pretty Georgian Gothic cottage with its end walls painted to look like church windows, was a popular haunt for river smugglers. Legend has it that a white cat was placed in the window as a signal to warn that the authorities had been alerted.

Turn left and proceed up the concrete marina road for about 300 yards passing boats laid up. Look out for a footpath sign on your left which at times can be partially hidden by boats. An attractive wooded path bears right and runs up the right-hand side of the valley to the edge of a clearing. It eventually emerges on to playing fields. Head for the left-hand corner of the churchyard.

Gilbert Scott's restoration work of 1862 has largely obliterated the medieval origins of St Michael's Church, which are basically 14th and 15th century. There are monuments to the Berners family who built the nearby hall, and also to Philip Bacon (1635).

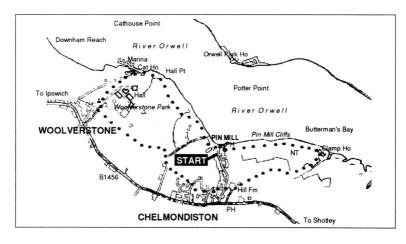

From the corner of the churchyard turn left and reach the metalled drive to Woolverstone Hall.

Woolverstone Hall was built in 1776 by William Berners, who was also responsible for Berners Street in London. His mother was a descendant of Cromwell. The Hall is now occupied by Ipswich High School. The 96 ft. high obelisk was erected in 1793 to commemorate Berner's death in 1783.

Turn right and take the second stile on your left. Walk through the park and cross stiles either side of the drive bordered by a new avenue of lime trees. Continue along a narrow path along the right side of a cultivated field with iron railings on your right and when you meet a track, carry straight on along it. Keep bearing right passing two houses until you reach another footpath. Turn right and head down the hill. Where the lane passes a pair of white wooden cottages, ignore the metalled track and take the footpath which leads steeply off to the left. You later cross a road and eventually arrive at Chelmondiston Church.

St Andrew's Church, enlarged 1868, rebuilt 1891, was virtually destroyed by a flying bomb in World War II. It has been uninspiringly rebuilt again.

Walk down the lane to the left of the church and arrive at the road which runs down to Pin Mill car park. (This allows the opportunity to cut short your walk here by turning left, but you will miss some great walking by doing so). Cross straight over and take the track opposite bearing left past farm buildings. The firm wide track heads between open fields with fine views of the river and eventually reaches Clamp House after passing to the left of an agricultural reservoir. When level with the house go left to locate a path which enters Pin Mill Cliff.

Thankfully Pin Mill Cliff is under the protection of The National Trust who acquired the woodland in 1978. It consists of woodland dominated by old Alder coppice. The slopes have been primarily colonised by sycamore with elm, hazel and a number of large oaks. On the other side of the footpath is a large soft wood plantation. Splendid views of the Orwell down below in Butterman's Bay and across to Levington Marina on the far bank present themselves through gaps in the trees.

You can take the path which goes immediately right down to the shore for a closer look before retracing your steps and setting off through the trees, the path gradually climbing to present spectacular views. Approaching Pin Mill again, the path drops to the shore as you pass a number of houseboats moored along the shore, each competing for its own personal identity. You leave the path by climbing steps in the bank on your left and continue behind houses. You break out into a close of houses and, walking to the end, descend steps bordered by metal handrails to the lane. Turn right back to the car park.

THE RIVER ORWELL
Walk 5: Trimley St Mary to Levington

Start:	*Leave the A14 Ipswich to Felixstowe road by the flyover to Trimley St Mary. In the village, park by the churchyard wall in the lane or on Trimley High Road in front of the church.*
O.S.Maps:	*Landranger 169; Pathfinder 1054.*
Distance:	*10 ½ miles.*
Refreshments:	*Three Mariners by the start and finish, or Levington Ship at half way.*
Description:	*The start of the walk is along fine firm tracks. You then skirt the new Felixstowe Port extension before setting off along the river bank, which is easy going except after wet weather when it can be sticky in places. From Levington Church your only section of road walking includes a steep hill climb from whence you proceed by track and field back to Trimley.*

CROSS THE ROAD and turn left. After about 150 yards, turn right down Gaymers Lane, a bridleway signposted 'River Orwell 1½ miles'.

Carefully cross the railway track and continue, now along a sunken green lane which swings left. At the end of the grazing meadow on your right, do not turn right to follow the footpath sign, but instead carry straight on for a few yards to meet a shingle track. Continue on this past houses to reach a metalled lane. Turn right and then bear right at a small triangular green to an information board introducing you to the Orwell and Trimley Marshes. Go through the entrance gates on to a wide metalled avenue bordered by young and established oaks. Later you leave the track, diverted right to skirt the high embankments thrown up by the Felixstowe Port extension. As you carry on you become aware of just how big a bite it has taken out of this sensitive area, an area acclaimed for its natural beauty and a haven for bird life.

Eventually the track bears left and you are able to climb the embankment to the river itself. The contrast to the sight that greeted me ten years ago, when the first River & Coastal book was planned, is stark. Then all was peace, just the call of the birds and the sound of the river lapping against the bank. Now massive ships stand against the new quays as cranes whine and clank their way back and forth from deck to shore, endlessly loading and unloading containers.

This is Fagbury Point. Turn right and commence your walk, the sounds of the river gradually taking over from those of industry and commerce and the sanctuary of Trimley Marshes, alive with birds and wildfowl, commencing over on your right.

The Orwell lies within Suffolk Coasts & Heaths Area of Outstanding Natural Beauty and the estuary is internationally important for its wintering wading birds and wildfowl. Suffolk Wildlife Trust's Trimley Marshes

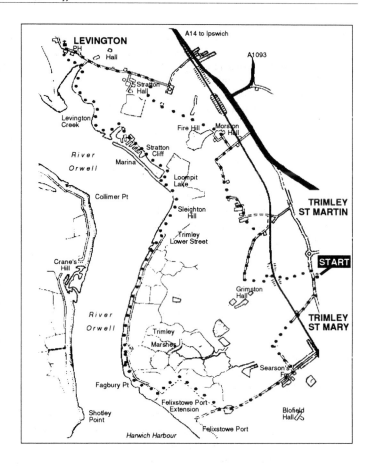

Nature Reserve provides an 84 hectare wetland reserve created from arable farmland in 1991 to mitigate the loss of inter-tidal habitat at Fagbury when the port was expanded along the estuary. The port funded the nature reserve, now one of the best in the county. The wetland supports many breeding avocet, redshank, lapwing and wintering gatherings of many species of wildfowl. The battle between nature and modern commercial progress is an ongoing one with worthy arguments on either side. Suffolk is justly proud of the achievements of its major port but equally aware of its duty to protect what nature has bestowed upon it. The give and take so far shown here suggests both camps can work together for the county's good. Unfortunately the question has to be asked, is this the end or just the beginning of a conflict of interests along this sensitive estuary.

After a walk of some 2 miles, the bank ends and you continue on a firm wide track climbing steeply through the trees up Sleighton Hill with lovely views of the river below and the ever closing marina at Levington. The track descends sharply and goes off right, but you continue straight on over a stile to walk a spectacular narrow causeway between the river and mudflats on the left and the lovely Loompit Lake with its many wildfowl on your right. Bear right as this well-worn path continues along the side of the inlet. At the end turn left to head towards the trees again where you start a lovely woodland walk climbing Stratton Cliff to pass the marina on your left. Eventually you reach and cross the marina access road via wooden gates. Continue on past sailing equipment shops and yachts in all shapes and sizes sporting names from the mundane to the impressively original. There are hundreds of boats moored here worth thousands: where on earth does all the money come from? Everybody to his own, but walking as an outdoor pastime certainly comes cheaper and no less satisfying for that!

The track ends and you are directed left across the grass with yachts to your left and lines of newly planted trees on your right to arrive back on the river bank.

Climb the wall and turn right to continue on beside the Orwell; part of the bank is quite new along this stretch and the land enclosed, only recently reclaimed. The route curves inland and then makes a positive right turn as you negotiate Levington Creek, once a popular haunt for smugglers. The bank is now replaced by a track and you head away from the main river course on this. At the end of the creek you have a choice. If you do not wish to visit the church or The Ship at Levington you can go through the gate ahead and walk along the drive to reach the road and turn right to pick up the full walk from *.

The full walk turns left just before the gate to continue on a path round the far side of the creek to a point where you enter a section of bushes and reach a metal part barrier. The river path continues on ahead to complete the circuit round the creek, but you turn right on another path through a canopy of bushes to come out at the bottom of a meadow. Ahead is the church tower and you set off up the meadow on a well-defined path to the top. At the end leave by a wooden gate and walk up a narrow path bordered by high hedges to come out on a country road opposite Levington Ship. Your route is right but take time here for a refreshment break and a visit to the church via a gate on the left.

> Remains of a vessel, apparently a Viking ship, thought to have belonged to a fleet which raided Ipswich in the 10th century, were found embedded in the mud in Levington Creek. The Levington Ship inn has a history of smuggling and intrigue, while the almshouses opposite were provided by Sir Robert Hitcham in 1636. It was Sir Robert who was responsible for the attractive late 15th century red brick tower of St Peter's Church.

You set off again down the winding road and, after the S bend, pass the track from the creek* and face a long haul up the hill past Stratton Hall before turning right down a drive to Suffolk Yacht Harbour (Levington Marina).

When you draw level with Stratton Hall Wood on your right, turn left on to a track heading up between cultivated fields. At the top carry straight on, picking up a hedge on your left and then heading steeply down hill. At the bottom you pass through a gateway and climb the short but very steep Fire Hill by a narrow path through heavy bracken. At the top continue on along the left side of a meadow. The wood away over on your right turns to meet you as you join a track leading to the farm ahead by a pond. At the farm buildings, go between a hay storage barn on the left and an implement shed on the right. Bear left, over a stile and bear right to walk past Morston Hall.

When the drive is crossed by a track, turn right along Hill Cottage Track and follow this left at a pillbox. You pass to the right of a pair of cottages and go down into woodland to cross a brook in front of a large red-brick building. Turn left here and take the earth track which bears right along a shady lane to emerge on a country lane opposite Goslings Cottage at Thorpe Common. Turn left and, ignoring the track which goes straight on by a footpath sign, follow the metalled lane right. At the end go over the grass and left by the transformer to follow the left side of the field on a grass path to the end of the garden boundary hedge on your left. Turn right here following a well-worn path into the cultivated field to the telegraph pole. Turn left and follow the line of the wires to the end of the field, still on a distinct path, to reach a country lane opposite a bungalow named Cherry Lynn. Turn right and walk past properties along Grimston Lane. Beyond the last on your left you reach a pair of cottages on your right. Leave the lane here by taking the footpath sign left across an open cultivated field - again you should see a distinct path created by other walkers. Pass to the right of a line of mature trees to reach the end of the field at a cross path. Turn left and walk to the end of the field on your right. Turn right and, with a hedge on your left, continue to the railway. Cross the track with care and continue ahead along Gun Lane, a wide grass path to a point where it forks. Bear left here and continue between open fields back to Trimley High Road. Turn right and walk back to the start by the two churches.

> The churches of St Martin, and St Mary with its ruinous west tower, stand side by side, their churchyards now merged together. Both are 14th century although St Martin's early origins are less well defined - its tower, nave and font having been modernised. The chapel of St Martin's Church was built by the will of Roger Cavendish in 1405 and there are other memorials to the family in both churches. A later Cavendish, Thomas, found fame as the second Englishman to sail round the world in 1588. He once owned Grimston Hall nearby, now a farmhouse.

The River Stour

For Stour, a daintie flood, that duly doth divide
Fair Suffolke from this shire upon her other side,
By Clare first coming in, and Sudbury doth show,
The even course she keepes; when farre she doth not flow,
But Breton a bright nymph, fresh succour to her brings:
Yet is she not so proud of her superfluous springs,
But Orwell coming in from Ipswitch thinkes that shee,
Should stand for it with Stour, and lastly they agree,
That since the Britans hence their first discoveries made,
And that into the east they first were taught to trade.
Besides, of all the roads, and havens of the east,
This harbour where they meet, is reckoned for the best.

(Michael Drayton)

IMMORTALISED by those two great Suffolk painters, John Constable and Thomas Gainsborough, the Stour formed the ancient division between the Kingdom of East Anglia and the county of Essex.

Although its source is in Cambridgeshire all its three tributaries, the Glem, the Box and the Brett, rise in Suffolk.

It is the county's largest river, being over one mile wide in places and fifty miles long - the last ten being tidal.

Its largest town is Sudbury but the Essex port of Harwich stands on the Orwell-Stour Estuary.

Wool was the greatest factor in the prosperity of the towns and villages which border the Stour, but this great East Anglian industry gradually declined through the latter half of the 16th century, and little has come since to replace it.

In the reign of Queen Anne an Act of Parliament in 1705 allowed for making the river navigable from Manningtree to Sudbury; the work started in 1708 and took five years. However, the trade it created was later lost to the railways.

Holbrook Creek (Walk 8)

THE RIVER STOUR
Walk 6: Haverhill to Kedington

Start: *Arriving in Haverhill on the A143 from Newmarket or Bury St Edmunds, turn left at the double roundabout. Carry on past the industrial estate, over the mini-roundabout and under the railway bridge. Turn left at the new roundabout just past the service station into Chalkstone Way and take the first turning right into Coupals Road. Park in the East Town Park Countryside Centre free car park on the right.*

O.S.Maps: *Landranger 154; Pathfinder 1028.*

Distance: *6½ miles.*

Refreshments: *Ketton House Tea Rooms and Barnardiston Arms, Kedington. There are a number of places in Haverhill itself.*

Description: *The walk starts along the disused railway track, then negotiates a large modern housing estate before breaking free into open countryside along firm tracks. Following a walk through the attractive village of Kedington with its ancient church, the route returns along field paths following the couse of the river Stour, and finally picking up the railway track again back to Haverhill.*

GO THROUGH THE WOODEN SWING GATE bearing right and left to head for a footbridge over the Stour Brook, a tributary of the River Stour. Climb the steps up the embankment on to the old disused railway track and turn right.

The Haverhill to Sudbury railway began in 1865 and completed 100 years in service. Although it survived the initial closures instigated by Beeching in the early '60s, the axe finally fell in 1967. Its resurrection as a recreational facility for walkers, especially those confined to a suburban environment, owes much to the foresight of the local councils and other authorities.

As you set off along this quiet tree-lined track set apart from the bustle of the busy town, you are directed by either footpath signs to Kedington or waymark arrows bearing the words 'Haverhill Country Walks' or 'Circular Walk'.
At a point where a new road has been cut through the embankment you must negotiate a stile and come down to cross Chalkstone Way. Continue on the far side, now on a concrete path. You pass an area of rough grassland, awaiting development, but in the meantime providing a rich habitat for insect, mammal and bird life. Later you cross Manor Road and return to the normal track path.
Leave the embankment immediately before the metal railway bridge by going down steps on the right by the footpath sign to Kedington.
Take the concrete path which heads up through an estate of modern houses. Pass

under the subway and head up the path either side of the wide grass strip between houses. The stiff climb terminates at another subway passing under Chalkstone Way where you emerge in the corner of a field.

Turn right and walk along the wide grass verge bordered by young trees parallel with the road. At the hedge continue beside the road along a wide verge and, just after the bus shelter, take the track going off left opposite Kingfisher Close.

The firm, wide track soon takes you out of sight and sound of Haverhill. Bear left of the wood heading down into a small valley where you cross a brook and climb up the far side towards Great Wilsey Farm. Pass between the first barns and to the right of the remainder along a rough grassy strip. At the end of the buildings turn right on what is initially a farm track then a wide grass track beside a field. This then heads between open cultivated fields with expansive views over the surrounding countryside. The tower of Kedington Church appears ahead as you make your way down the valley towards the village.

You eventually arrive at the road. Cross over and head along Mill Road. Opposite Stourmead Close - the entrance to the old Risbridge Hospital, and once the village workhouse - a footpath sign directs you to the right side of the hedge to walk along the left side of a small playing field. At the river you may decide, especially if it's a fine day, to take a break beside the water in this attractive setting. Return to the road and cross the bridge over the Stour. An arm of the river has been diverted to run under what was originally the old water mill on your right, now converted into a home. Head up to the church.

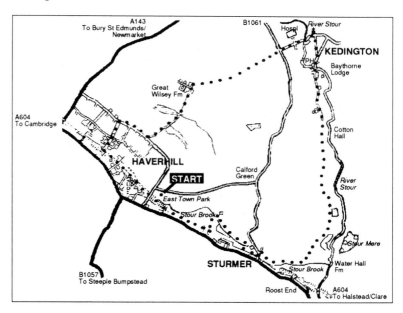

You need time to explore the wonders of St Peter & St Paul, a monument to the Barnardiston family with no less than nine men and women and eight children featured in stone. The immense atmosphere here represents an amalgamation of all the periods of history from the Roman building which lies beneath the floor, the Anglo-Saxon cross from c900, the fine low-pitched Tudor roof to the box pews and 18th century gallery.

Return to the road by the far gate and cross over to enter Church Walk, an avenue of limes and horse chestnuts, heading towards the school. Cross the brook carried from your left in a deep ravine before arriving at West End Lane. Turn right passing Ketton House Antiques and Tea Room, a possible refreshment stop.
At the junction keep on in the direction of Haverhill, past the Spa shop, and cross the Stour again to enter Silver Street. The river is very impressive here. Just over the bridge the road bends right and you leave it to carry straight on to the left of the Barnardiston Arms, named after the former Lords of the Manor and your last chance of liquid refreshment.

Another notable family in Kedington were the Sainsburys who owned much of the property in the village centre and several farms around.
The next section of the walk is on the Stour Valley Path, a long distance footpath which runs for 60 miles from Newmarket to the estuary at Cattawade. Although you are never within touching distance of the river, you follow its course as far as Stour Mere.

At first you have playing fields between yourself and the Stour on your left and unfortunately it is some way before you even catch a glimpse of the water. Pass the delightful Ketton Thatch (Ketton is the former name for Kedington) and beyond the sewage works the way becomes unmetalled, later reducing to a well-walked path beside open cultivated fields.
You continue on for some distance with the occasional plank bridge to cross. Although this section of the route may appear rather bland, it probably dates from pre-Roman times. Later the river becomes more obvious especially at Stour Mere, a large expanse of water created by the river flood. Unfortunately it is at this point that you leave the Stour to join Stour Brook. At the end of the field on your right, pass through a gap in the hedge and take the right fork as the path divides. Walk diagonally across the field to reach trees on the far side to the right of the footbridge. Here you meet a five-fingered footpath sign and leave the Stour Valley Path by taking the path through the trees beside a high bank; the brook is through the trees on the left. Pass Challice Barn and Farm House to reach the road at Sturmer, on the Essex side of the border, on a bend.

Sturmer is famous for the Sturmer Pippin apple which local nurseryman Ezekiel Dillestone first recorded in 1831. His descendants took it to Australia and New Zealand since when large numbers are now exported.

Turn left and then right just before the road bridge to pick up a length of disused railway track, the same track on which you set out earlier. This crosses the brook by a metal bridge and, following this, you have an alternative. You can either keep on ahead along the old track or go over the footbridge on the right and then turn left to walk along the grassy path through water meadows, and later beside the brook to join the railway track further on.

If you wish to take the latter route, then cross the footbridge, turn left and walk through the meadow on a faint path through rough grass. At a post and rail fence turn left to enable you to actually walk by the bank of the brook, although this is rather uneven. You eventually arrive at impressive white entrance gates to Pope Mill Farm and turn left over the footbridge to walk along a metalled drive through a golf course - watch your head! As you approach the railway bridge, do not climb with the track but instead take the path running parallel on the left side of the trees. At the end go down the steps back on to the old railway track to join those who have opted for the direct route. Turn right and pass under the bridge.

> You pass derelict osier willow beds on your left that once provided the supple shoots used by a Haverhill firm of basket makers. These were cut by hand, stripped off the bark and woven into a variety of containers. The Borough Council has begun to cut the old stumps (known as Stools) to rejuvenate them. New shoots grow as much as six feet the following year!

Ignore the first footpath sign directing you off the track on the right and take the second at the point you originally joined it, negotiating the steps down the embankment, recrossing the footbridge and returning to the car park.

THE RIVER STOUR
Walk 7: Stratford St Mary, East Bergholt & Flatford

Start: *Take the slip road to Dedham off the A12 Ipswich - Colchester road and turn right to park by Stratford St Mary Church.*

O.S.Maps: *Landranger 155 & 168; Pathfinder 1053.*

Distance: *8 miles.*

Refreshments: *There are pubs in East Bergholt, a Tea Room at Flatford Mill and pubs and restaurants in Dedham just off the walk.*

Description: *The walk sets off through farmland above the Stour Valley to East Bergholt, then takes a country lane and tracks to Flatford Mill. The last section is along well-used paths by the banks of the river Stour, passing Dedham over on the Essex side and ending with a lengthy walk along a metalled drive running parallel with the A12 back to the church.*

WALK BACK TO THE JUNCTION and turn left. After a few yards go right to set off along a footpath through open fields. Pick up the field edge at the end running parallel with a farm track on your right. At the end of the field join this track and carry straight on passing a reservoir over on your right. Continue up the hill with lovely views across the Dedham Vale. Cross over Deadmans Lane and carry on ahead along a well-used path by the left side of a cultivated field. You head down on a wide grassy path and at the bottom of the dip follow the field boundary right for a few yards before dropping down to a gravel drive.

Cross over and after negotiating a footbridge and stile, walk up the right side of the green. At the top join a metalled lane. You pass properties including the Congregational Church to reach the road by the post office in East Bergholt. There is a pub just to the left, but your way is to cross the road and turn right. Within a few paces you reach John Constable's birthplace.

It was here in East Bergholt and the Dedham Vale that Constable found his inspiration to become one of England's finest landscape painters. He wrote "I even love every stile and stump and every lane in the village". Regretfully the house is gone and replaced by little more than a plaque to his memory bearing the dates 1776-1837, but many of the views he painted and admired remain as they were today for us also to enjoy.

A few steps further brings us to East Begholt's unique church.

A mass of windows and battlements, turrets and doorways, St Mary's Church is eminently impressive and picturesque both inside and out. The unusual detached bell tower is probably unique in England and no doubt

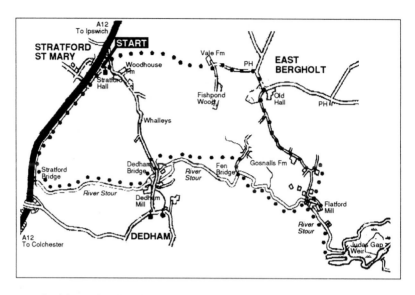

resulted from the abandonment of the west tower which had been part of a massive investment in the church by Cardinal Wolsey during the height of his power but ended, alas, on his sudden fall from grace.

At the bend, cross the road to the memorial and go right along a narrow metalled lane with 'No Entry' signs. There are fine views from seated viewpoints across to Stratford St Mary Church, a popular scene in many of Constable's paintings. At a point where another lane goes off right, you carry straight on with the option of walking along a narrow path on the left side of the hedge with a fenced meadow on your left, keeping parallel with the lane. (This route is particularly preferable in summer when the narrow lane can be busy with tourist traffic.)

When the lane crosses a stream you join it again enclosed by high banks. Walk on past the National Trust car park bearing left with the road and ignoring the lane bearing right to Flatford. The road climbs, and at a point where it levels off and straightens, look for a signpost where you go over a stile on the right. Head diagonally down the field to another stile on the far side. Pick up a well-used path along the right side of a field, with views of the Stour to your left snaking its way through water meadows, and the famous Willy Lott's Cottage being the second building from the left in the distance ahead. The path swings right and left to continue along the left side of the next field down to the lane.

Turn left to pass Granary Barn with its Museum which is open to the public. Continue on to the Field Centre and Willy Lott's Cottage.

Flatford Mill, Mill House and Willy Lott's Cottage were purchased in 1943 by The National Trust together with 16 acres of surrounding land. The Mill House is now a centre where students are taught the rudiments of natural history. The Mill belonged to the painter's father, and John worked for a year here. Willy Lott's Cottage, one of Constable's most popular works, was once the home of a Willy Lott who is said to have lived there for more than eighty years without ever leaving it for more than four days.

Retrace your steps and continue on to the National Trust Gift Shop and Tea Garden for souvenirs and refreshments.
Cross the river Stour by the footbridge and, if you have the energy, turn left for a short detour to see Flatford Mill and on to Lower Barn Farm and Judas Gap Weir. Return to the bridge and this time carry straight on along the left bank of the river for some way through open water meadows interspersed with willows.
You eventually arrive at a large impressive wooden footbridge and take this to cross the river. Head away on a track, through a metal farm gate and along a shady track. A path comes in from the left to join you and you turn left to follow it, going almost back on yourself between high hedges.
You leave the hedged path by a kissing gate and continue through an open meadow gradually converging on the river again, this time on the right bank. Reach the road by another kissing gate. Go left over the road bridge and leave it by going right through a third kissing gate to gradually pick up the river bank again opposite Dedham Mill. Look for a point where a well-worn path begins beside the river and you can leave the meadow to join it. Go through yet another kissing gate and on through water meadows, continuing to follow the right bank of the Stour.
You eventually reach the end of the meadow and the meandering river at a point where the busy A12 is carried over the river. Follow the footpath sign right - do not go under the bridge - and pick up a gravel drive running parallel with, and below the main road.
Continue along this drive for some distance still parallel with the A12 with Stratford St Mary Church ahead. Eventually you pass to the left of Stratford Hall farm and reach the road. Turn right and walk the few paces back to the church and your starting point.

St Mary's, ungraciously isolated from the main village by the construction of the Stratford St Mary bypass, is mainly 16th century. Although considerably restored, there remains much of interest. The North aisle and chapel were built in 1499 by Thomas and Margaret Mors, and the porch two years later. William Dowsing, who did such irreparable damage to Suffolk's churches, is said to have been born in the parish.

THE RIVER STOUR
Walk 8: Erwarton, Harkstead & Lower Holbrook

Start:	*Take the B1456 from Ipswich to Shotley passing under the Orwell Bridge. Just into Shotley take the right turn signposted 'Erwarton Walk'. At the T-junction opposite Erwarton Hall turn right and park in the unmade lane beside Erwarton Church.*
O.S.Maps:	*Landranger 169; Pathfinder 1053 & 1054.*
Distance:	*9 miles.*
Refreshments:	*The Queen's Head, Erwarton and The Baker's Arms, Harkstead.*
Description:	*The first half of the walk comprises easy walking on firm, wide tracks, with the occasional field edge followed by a rather long section across open fields to Lower Holbrook, and the second half follows the Stour, usually with the choice of either a well-worn path along the field edge - often elevated on the cliff above the river - or beside the river itself on a sand and shingle 'beach'.*

SET OFF ALONG ERWARTON STREET passing properties on either side. Immediately past the last cottage on the right, turn right to walk along the right side of a large cultivated field. At the end of the field continue on through the next following the field boundary which gradually bears left. You arrive on a firm track on a bend but must immediately leave it to go through the gap in the hedge on the right by a footpath sign.

One finger directs you to the right of New Covert on a grassy strip between open fields, but your route is diagonally across the open field passing to the left of the covert. However, it would seem sensible that if the wide grassy area has still been left unploughed running parallel with the hedge on your left, you proceed on this round the field to end in the far left hand-corner.

Here you meet another track leading to Crouch House and this one you follow. After passing Rosemary Cottage the track swings left but after a few paces you leave it to walk over the field on your left in line with the telegraph poles. At the hedge turn left and, still following telegraph poles, walk along the bottom of the field with a hedge and high bank on your right bearing left towards the line of firs ahead. Here you meet a track and turn right passing the buildings of Rence Park Farm. Cross over another track and keep on ahead. Later you skirt a cottage and join a lane. (Note that the old signpost points left to Shotley and Arwarton, the old name for Erwarton.) Carry on and go left at the T-junction to reach Harkstead Church.

The fine 15th century tower is a prominent feature of St Mary's Church which is mainly constructed of local septaria. Most of the rest of the church is 14th century but there is evidence of Norman work in windows on the north side of the aisle and a blocked doorway.

Come back out of the churchyard and turn right to walk to the end of the wall. Turn right by the letter-box and go over a stile into a grazing meadow. Walk along the right side and cross a metal farm gate and stile to walk between post and rail fencing. At the end cross two further stiles leading you into a cultivated field. Turn right for a few yards into the corner then left parallel with the road to an opening in the hedge and a farm track.

Turn left and walk along this track between open fields down into the valley. Continue up the far side over a metal gate and over a stile beside another gate. Pass to the left of The Vale Farm and follow the track right skirting the gardens. Reach the main concrete farm drive and turn left on to it to reach a country road.

Turn right along Ipswich Road and after a short distance go through a gap in the hedge into the field on your left by a footpath sign. Turn half right and head across the open field. After about 200 yards, stop and turn left. Now head across the remainder of the field to the far left hand corner. Go through the hedge and out on to a dirt track on a bend. Cross straight over the track and continue diagonally over the next field in roughly the same direction as before to the far corner. Go through the hedge again to be confronted with yet another open field to cross. Head to the right of a clump of trees in the middle and then turn slightly right to descend, making for the end of the hedgeline on the right. Go through into the field on the right here and walk along the boundary parallel with the road over on your left bordered by modern bungalows. At the elbow where the hedge ends follow it left and then go right and left round the garden boundary to reach the road beside Broom Cottage.

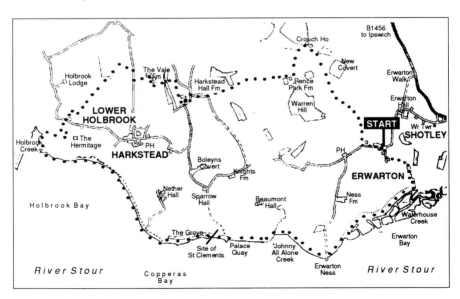

Go a few steps right then take the footpath sign left along a track which becomes a well-worn path climbing surprisingly steeply up the left side of a cultivated field. Follow the boundary hedge left and right. At the crossways of paths turn right and walk across the field with stunning views across the Stour at Holbrook Bay and the impressive tower at the Royal Hospital School ahead. The path descends to join a track at the bottom where you turn left; this is Holbrook Creek.

At the head of the creek are the remains of mud berths and wooden wharves. These were used by sailing barges which took hay and straw, produced on local farms, to London to be used as fodder and bedding for horses. A common return cargo was 'muck', the sweepings of the London stables, to fertilise the Suffolk fields.

Climb the river wall and turn left to commence the walk along the Stour back to Erwarton. At the hedge switch to the path along the field edge; this well-worn path will take you all the way back along the river, often elevated on cliffs above the Stour with superb views across the water. However, at low tide, the section past the trees is best appreciated along the foreshore so, at the first tree you reach, go down the bank on your right on a path taking you down to the sand and shingle 'beach' and set off along the foreshore, negotiating the fallen trees.

At high tide most of the beach is under water, but at low tide the mud flats are revealed. They prove vital to the survival of large numbers of wildfowl such as wigeon, shelduck and brent geese as well as wading birds including grey plover, ringed plover, redshank, oystercatcher, black-tailed godwit, curlew and dunlin. It is for this reason that the Nature Conservation Council have designated the Stour Estuary a Site of Special Scientific Interest.

The estuary is popular for sailing although sailors need a good knowledge of the channel if they are to avoid going aground on the mud. Trading vessels can sometimes be seen heading for, or leaving, the small port of Mistley, 3 miles up the estuary on the Essex side. On the Essex shore opposite Holbrook Bay is Wrabness.

Leave the foreshore to pick up the field path just beyond the point where you cross a small stream; from hereon you stay with the path. A mile and a half of enjoyable walking from Holbrook Bay takes you to a position opposite Copperas Bay.

Copperas, a less common name for ferrous sulphate, was a material which looked similar to small pieces of twig. In earlier days it was dug from the cliffs and used as a dye, colour wash for cottage exteriors and as an ink.

The site of St Clements Church lies in the corner of the field which ends at a point

where you need to cross another path heading away from the river to Sparrow Hall. Go a few steps left before negotiating a cross hedge. Before proceeding, look over the cliff just into the next field where you will see the remains of Palace Quay.

St Clements Church, of which nothing now remains, was mentioned at the time of Domesday. It was also mentioned in 1540 as being a chapel dedicated to St Clement. A neat layer of septaria stone marks the site of the old Palace Quay which would likely have been associated with the chapel.

The intriguingly named Johnny All Alone Creek, where you pass Beaumont Hall over on your left, forces you back from the river, and after rounding Erwarton Ness, an extensive area of marsh and mud flats at Waterhouse Creek takes the path on a raised river bank round the inlet. Parkeston Quay can be seen on the far bank, while ahead, on the estuary, the dock cranes at Harwich. As you proceed, the church back at Erwarton becomes clearer, an encouragement to tired limbs. It is not until you are past it and the sweep of Erwarton Bay commences its turn back to the river that you reach a culvert across a stream. Do not cross it but instead take the track inviting you to leave the delights of the Stour and head away along the right side of a cultivated field. The field boundary goes left and right and at the end go over a footbridge partly hidden in the trees on your left. Carry on to the end of this field and turn left. After a few paces a waymark arrow sends you right of the hedge and on towards a cottage. Walk through a small meadow heading for the corner where a wooden gate takes you out into the lane to the right of the cottage. Head up the lane and walk through the churchyard to visit Erwarton Church before returning to your starting point.

Septaria is again the main building material used for St Mary's Church, giving it a rather mellow appearance. Its haunting location; its associations with the Boleyn family - a casket discovered during restoration work in 1836 is said to contain Anne Boleyn's heart - and the ancient monuments in the south aisle of a medieval knight (1287), and another of a knight and lady (c1330), would be expected to create a rather austere atmosphere within. The light, bright and spacious interior therefore comes as something of a surprise.

Details of Erwarton Hall, which you pass on your way to and from Erwarton, will be included in another walk to be published in Volume II.

THE RIVER STOUR
Walk 9: From Sudbury by 'River and Rail'

Start: *From the double roundabout in the centre of Sudbury follow the sign to the leisure centre and station. Turn left to the station just prior to the leisure centre car park and drive to the far end of the station car park.*

O.S.Maps: *Landranger 155; Pathfinder 1029.*

Distance: *5½ miles.*

Refreshments: *There are plenty of opportunities for refreshments in Sudbury town but none on the walk except for the Tarantella, a high-class restaurant which you pass during your brief excursion on to the busy A31 on the outskirts of town.*

Description: *A surprisingly fine river walk on a well planned, well signposted, winding route from the centre of Sudbury to meet the old disused railway track at Borley Mill. The return journey is straight back along the track. The going is flat and very easy.*

AT THE FAR END OF THE CAR PARK a path bordered by a high ivy-clad wooden fence leads you to a track beside white gates. Turn right and carry on to join a firm path at Friars Meadow. Turn right on this to enter the meadow and set off beside the river Stour. Over on your right is the embankment of the disused railway track on which you will return.

> The water meadows, the oldest recorded in East Anglia, were first mentioned by name in the latter part of the 12th century although they probably pre-date the Norman Conquest. In the mid-13th century Richard de Clare, Earl of Gloucester & Hereford gave the area of Portmanscroft and King's Marsh to the Burgesses of Sudbury for 'Forty shillings of silver' to be paid at the Feast of St Michael each year. Now managed for the Freemen of Sudbury by Trustees, the common lands are a designated Local Nature Reserve reflecting their importance.

At the end of the meadow follow the inlet of the river right and go under the railway bridge spanning the water for a short detour of a few yards.

> On the far side of the water is the Quay Theatre. The building has served many purposes since being built as a granary warehouse over 200 years ago. It once served as the town's first power station. A cable was taken from the station and linked from house to house and back again rather on the principle of Christmas tree lights. It was said that "If somebody removed a bulb on the Market Place the whole ruddy town went out!"

The Stour Navigation, set up in 1705 came up to Sudbury and the barges, known as lighters (one is preserved here) berthed in the Quay Basin and at other wharfs in the area. The Navigation lighters carried local produce to the seaports of Manningtree and Mistley for transportation to London by sailing barge. They brought back coal and fertilisers. Bricks were manufactured at Ballingdon and a number of granaries were used. Although the railways began taking their business from their opening in 1849 the Company continued to trade until 1935.

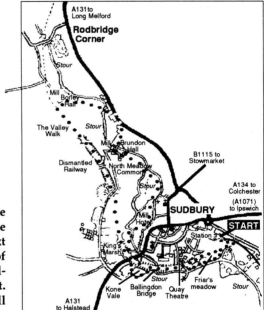

Retrace your steps and climb the embankment to walk along the disused railway track to the next bridge. Come down at the end of that bridge and pick up a well-walked path which forks left. Continue in an arc round a small Nature Reserve known as Kone Vale. You cross two plank footbridges along the way and when you come to an area of green continue bearing right. As you approach information boards and the embankment again, fork left towards houses and out into Ballingdon Street.

Go under Ballingdon Bridge and cross the busy road with care. Go through the new entrance gates opposite and pass information boards prior to entering King's Marsh along with North Meadow Common beyond are further sections of the extensive common lands. Walk diagonally over to the footbridge and from here converge on the main river in front of Mill Hotel. Go through the gate and turn left to pass to the left of the hotel and then set off along the left bank of the Stour.

The industrial history of the area is reflected in the number of water mills. Ballingon Mill (now Mill Hotel) is one of four between Sudbury and Long

Melford. It was converted in the early 1970s and has its lounge bar built around the original water wheel which, although not in use, still turns. Your route will take you past Brundon Mill which dates back to the 18th century, but stands on the site of an earlier mill, and Borley Mill.

You proceed on a raised tow path and go over sluice gates. Beyond the river at the wooden footbridge is Acton Square dominated by St Peter's Church.
Beyond the next concrete footbridge is the site of the old Edwardian Bathing Place last used in the 1930s. The metalled path ends here and you come out on to the Common but stay along the river bank to the end. Turn left and cross the bridge at the end by an impressive weir. Pass to the right of the pillbox to continue along the river bank before crossing a wooden footbridge and stile over a dry stream bed. Head towards the brick wall in front of the red-brick Georgian Brundon Hall. Go over a stile by the flint cottage and along the track past Hill Cottage. At the T-junction turn right signposted 'Melford Road' and cross the bridge by Brundon Mill. Carry on along the metalled drive out on to the A131.
Turn left and walk past the Tarantella Restaurant and leave the road by the end of the speed limit sign by taking a footpath down beside Holgate Cottage. Cross the bridge, go through a kissing gate and turn right to pick up the river bank again. You pass to the left of Borley Hall and Mill to reach the old railway track. Turn left and follow the delightful Valley Walk along the disused track back to Sudbury.

The Railway Age reached Sudbury on 2nd July 1849 when the first train arrived from Colchester. The line became part of the Eastern Counties Railway Company in 1860 and the Great Eastern two years later. In 1865 the line was extended to join the London to Cambridge at Shelford and the branch line from Long Melford to Bury St Edmunds opened on the same day. Three trains each way between Sudbury and Bury every weekday rose to six by 1914, a level it maintained until the 1950s. Heavy goods traffic between Cambridge and Colchester used this line in preference to the Colne Valley or Clare-Haverhill routes, especially during the War. The line finally closed in March 1967. Three sections were purchased by the West Suffolk County Council in the early '70s to provide the public with countryside walks that were clearly defined, easily traversed and safe from traffic. The walks are not public rights of way and are subject to Byelaws which are displayed at the main entrances.

When you are level with Somerfields Supermarket over on your left, leave the old track by crossing a footbridge by the Friar's Meadow signboard. Take the path diagonally over the meadow to reach the path on which you set out. After a few steps fork off left across a grassy path and leave the meadow by a metal footbridge. Turn left and walk back to the car park.

44

The River Deben

No stately villas, on thy side,
May be reflected in thy tide;
No lawn like parks, outstretching round,
The willing loiterer's footsteps bound
By woods, that cast their leafy shade,
Or deer that start across the glade;
No ruin'd abbey, grey with years,
Upon thy marge its pile uprears;
Nor crumbling castle, valour's hold,
Recalls the feudal days of old.

Nor dost thou need that such should be,
To make thee, Deben, dear to me:
Thou hast thy own befitting charms,
Of quiet heath and fertile farms,
With here and there a copse to fling
Its welcome shade, where wild birds sing;
Thy meads, for flocks and herds to graze;
Thy quays and docks, where seamen raise
Their anchor, and unfurl their sail
To woo and win the favouring gale.

(Bernard Barton)

RISING in Aspal near Debenham, the Deben fails to reach river status until it reaches Woodbridge; it is from here to the sea that all its ancient settlements lie. The lower part of the Deben once formed the great open port of Goseford, the wool port of the Saxons.

While the Orwell may always have been the main entry point for invasion, the provocative atmosphere of the Deben proved the major attraction when it came to ancient settlement. The estuary is still haunted by the Wuffingas, the ruling house of Saxon East Anglia at the time when pagan rites were being slowly superceded by Christian. The great Sutton Hoo treasure ship burial dates from this time.

There were many ancient quays along the banks of the river. Though none were large, they combined to make the Deben a thriving source of trade. Salt was manufactured at Hemley in salt pans both here and across the river at Sutton; cement, created from a mixture of river mud and chalk at Waldringfield until a few years before the First World War (subsequently new methods were learned from Germany and the works moved to Claydon where it still operates today). Ramsholt had a thriving oyster industry and, as stated earlier, coprolite was discovered by the shore and many quays set up to handle its shipping, Stonner Quay being one of the largest.

Woodbridge, where the river really began in earnest, took over from Goseford as the main port in the 15th century, but with the Deben being unnavigable for larger ships, soon lost all its trade to Ipswich. It accepted its destiny gracefully and remains a picturesque yachting centre.

Evening on the Deben (Walk 11)

THE RIVER DEBEN
Walk 10: Martlesham to Woodbridge

Start:	*Take the A1214 (the old A12) to Martlesham from the southern end of the Woodbridge bypass. At the bottom of the hill park in the layby just past the Red Lion.*
O.S.Maps:	*Landranger 169; Pathfinder 1031.*
Distance:	*6 ½ miles.*
Refreshments:	*The Red Lion at Martlesham and several just off the walk in Woodbridge.*
Description:	*Fine country walking with just a short length of quiet country road to Seckford Hall. You cross the busy A12 and negotiate your way through the outskirts of Woodbridge before the delightful river side walk to Kyson Point and Martlesham Creek, finishing on a lovely woodland path.*

SET OFF ALONG THE ROAD heading away from the Red Lion. Turn left into Post Office Lane by a group of cottages. The track becomes rough and uneven before reaching a footbridge and stile leading into a cultivated field. Cross the field and the railway track beyond via a stile on either side. Cross another cultivated field to reach the Woodbridge bypass carrying the busy A12 away from the town. As you cross the field note the impressive 5-arched railway bridge over to your left. At the end of the field go a few yards left down to a point where a farm track takes you under the road.

Emerge on the other side and take the track right, bearing left at the boundary of the golf course. Skirting higher ground on the right you continue along the side of the valley with lovely views across the busy A12 back to Martlesham.

Pass a cottage and farm buildings to join a metalled lane. The way divides and you take the one forking right and climbing past a modern bungalow. When you reach a quiet country road turn right and walk the half mile to Seckford Hall.

Seckford Hall was built between 1553 and 1585 by Woodbridge's great benefacter, Sir Thomas Seckford, Master of Requests to Elizabeth I. After a long period of neglect it was purchased by Sir Ralph Harwood in the late 1940s and it was he who skilfully restored it to its former glory and opened it as an hotel. This it remains today with a reputation befitting its station.

Turn left opposite the hotel entrance along a sandy track beside the golf course. The track ends at Wood Barn Cottages where you carry straight on along a grassy path between open fields interspersed with mature oaks. At the end of the field turn right for a few yards, then left through a hedge. Continue along the right side of a meadow, hedge on right, and at the end go over a stile on the right to walk along a well-worn path along the left side of a field with a high hedge on your left. At the end turn right onto a wide dirt track, then almost immediately left passing to the left of a cottage and heading down a narrow shady path by the converted Gazebo Barn. Come out to meet the busy A12 again and cross the dual-carriageway with care.

Go through a gap in the hedge in line with the path you came out on the other side and walk away along Bilney Road in the same direction as before. Turn left into Naunton Road, then immediately right down Colletts Walk. Beyond the green square at the bottom continue on along the metalled path between properties. At the end of the attractive flint and tile wall on your left, come out into Seckford Street.

Carry straight on past the impressive Seckford Hospital. At the end of the park on the right, go down the steps bordered by white railings to walk along the left side of the park. At the end where a path joins you from the right, the way bears left between hedges. At Cumberland Street turn right to pass Notcutt's Garden Centre and then turn off left down Cherry Tree Road. As you approach the bottom you catch your first glimpse of the Deben. Cross straight over Kingston farm Road and head diagonally left over the recreation ground bearing left of the tennis courts. Carry on to the far left-hand corner where you join a lane. Carry on down, cross the railway track and climb the promenade to the river.

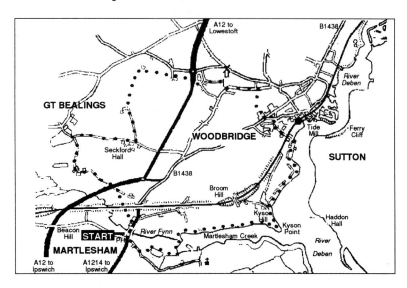

Over to your left is the well-photographed Tide Mill, one of only a handful left in England. Records show that there has been a tide mill here since at least 1170. The present mill was probably built in the early 18th century and was working until 1956 when the shaft of the 20 feet diameter water wheel broke. It was restored in 1968 and is open to the public daily in summer, weekends in October and at the warden's discretion in winter.

On the far side of the river is the site of Sutton Hoo comprising 11 burial mounds. In the largest, in 1939, Basil Brown unearthed the famous ship-burial. The treasure it contained still remains Britain's greatest collection from the Anglo-Saxon period.

Benches allow you the opportunity of a short break to relax and enjoy the peace and beauty of the river. If it is summer the river will be alive with noise and colour. Expanses of moody mudflats, cries of the gulls and the regular clanking of rigging on boats at their moorings create in winter a haunting but no less appealing atmosphere.

Turn right and set off along the promenade passing Deben Yacht Club. When this ends continue along the well-worn river path.

Looking over the river and the water meadows there are a wide variety of common plants to be seen, with poppies, hawkbits and reeds found on the banks.

Eventually you reach Kyson Hill an area of woodland which is maintained by the National Trust. Go through the trees and bear left down to the waterside. Carry on beside the river to the end at Kyson Point where another path goes off right to Martlesham, skirting Martlesham Creek.

No evidence remains of the Saxon settlement recorded at Kyson Point, but it was used as a quay in Victorian times. In the peace and solitude of Martlesham Creek you may see swans, gulls, dragonflies and shelduck and many different waders. The meadows over on your right are the growing centre for Notcutt's Nurseries.

The path is fenced on the river side at first and often sticky. It then climbs to run, rather unevenly, along the elevated river bank. You eventually pass around the end of the creek and go over a stile to enter a wood. After a few yards turn right. Go over the footbridge on the right and turn left. This delightful walk through woodland, dotted with superb mature oaks, eventually ends and you carry on beside a grazing meadow to reach a lane. Turn right and walk back to the Red Lion and your starting point.

THE RIVER DEBEN
Walk 11: Waldringfield to Hemley

Start:	*Take the Waldringfield turning off the A12 at the Brightwell Corner roundabout south of Martlesham. The road goes sharp right into Waldring-field, then left. Take the right turning to the church and, if there is space, park on the village hall car park.*
O.S.Maps:	*Landranger 169; Pathfinder 1031.*
Distance:	*6½ miles.*
Refreshments:	*The Maybush down on Waldringfield Quay and The Fox Inn, Newbourne.*
Description:	*The outward journey is by field and path via Newbourne and Hemley down to Kirton Creek. Unfortunately, a major break in the river wall - which is still unlikely to be resolved by your visit - necessitates a return to Hemley (albeit by a circular route) and an alternative path inland via Hemley Hall and White Hall to rejoin the river walk just prior to Waldringfield. While this does cut out a considerable stretch of river walking, the replacement tracks provide good easy walking with lovely views of the river throughout.*

WALK BACK UP MILL ROAD and take the footpath left between high hedges. (You return by the path going off on the other side of the road.) Follow the left side of a field then pass through a canopy of hedges. At the stile break out of the trees and carry on across an open cultivated field to reach a country lane on a bend. Carry on passing a small wood on your left and after a short distance the lane bears left and you leave it to carry straight on across an open field along a faint path. At the end swing right by the gas marker to enter the edge of a wood. The overgrown path drops steeply into a valley snaking round fallen trees and nettly undergrowth. Pass to the left of an Eastern Electricity substation enclosed by wooden fencing and come out on a narrow road. Turn right into Newbourne.

A Government scheme in 1930 to help unemployed Yorkshire and Durham miners led to the sectioning off of much of Newbourne to create the Newbourne Estate. Each unit consisted of a small house of standard size and design, two glasshouses and a plot of land to grow flowers and vegetables. Today most of these smallholdings are in the hands of local Suffolk people.

Carry on past the turning to Martlesham and the Nature Reserve. The road goes over a stream and passes the Fox Inn and pretty Chapel Cottage bearing left. The church is over on your right.

St Mary's Church has a fine Decorated tower. An extension to the South

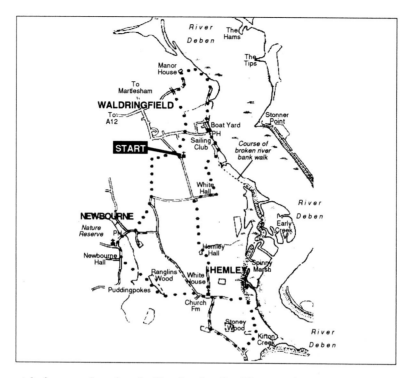

aisle forms a chapel to the Rowley family. The nave has a hammerbeam roof, while the piscina and a stone coffin lid provide evidence of the church's 13th and 14th century origins.

Continue along the street bearing left into Mill Road where you pass the lovely walled Newbourne Hall.

This is a timber-framed hallhouse of c1500, enlarged around 1612. A fine 14th century doorway once led to a chapel. It seems to have originally been built round a courtyard but only two sides now remain.

Immediately past the village hall turn left over the concrete parking area and walk down the right hand side of the meadow through rough grass to locate a footpath sign at the bottom. Continue on through marshy ground going diagonally right and passing to the left of a single tree and then left of a small copse to cross a stream. Go over a stile into a meadow and follow a faint path diagonally right and then through a second, smaller meadow. Bear left and right into a third, a path heads for the far left hand corner where you find a metal farm gate. Go through and up the left side of a large cultivated field on a grassy path. From the end of the field

where you join a farm track, look back at the view over the valley. From here you can see the Newbourne smallholdings with their glasshouses.

At the end of the wood on your left the track turns left and you follow it in the direction of the church ahead. You now get your first views of the Deben to your left. You reach the road and arrive at Hemley Church.

> Except for its fine red-brick 15th century west tower, the original 13th century church of All Saints was practically rebuilt in 1889.

Just past the church turn right into a green lane which slowly bears left over some distance. Eventually you reach the river wall at the end of the trees on your left and climb it. This is Kirton Creek. During the Middle Ages there was a ferry service between the creek and Ramsholt on the opposite bank. Turn left to skirt the creek and reach the river proper. Shortly you arrive at a point where the bank is overgrown and you are confronted by a sign notifying you of a break in the river wall some 400 metres ahead. I can confirm that the break is dramatic and totally impassable so unless some provision has been made to restore the link by the time you complete this walk - which seems very unlikely - you must turn left here and take the path which leads back to Hemley. Before doing so, if you have energy to spare, you can continue on ahead along the overgrown river bank, or the level (but marshier) ground beside it, until you reach the break, then retrace your steps back to this junction.

Either way you now turn left along the path and then join a green lane which leads you to a firm stony farm track which takes you right, past the buildings and back to the road. Turn left on the road to pass Hemley Church again and take the turning right. Follow this country lane with lovely views across to the Deben on your right. Just past Hemley Hall Cottages the lane ends at a farm gate. Carry straight on, now on a wide track. You reach the farm and pass over the concrete yard to continue ahead along another firm track. You eventually reach a narrow country lane on a bend. Turn right to walk down a shady green lane, passing Whitehall Cottage, which develops into a grassy track as it passes White Hall. Turn left at the end of the garden and follow a track through open cultivated fields with views of the river. Later you pass between pools and go right to skirt another larger one on your right down a meandering path via a stile and moored yachts to finally arrive at the Deben.

Turn left along the waterfront past chalets and the sailing club at delightful Waldringfield. You pass the Maybush pub, a possible refreshment stop on your left in Quay Road, and just beyond Deben Cruises and Chandlers take the narrow path right beside a hedge just before the private road back to the quay. Turn left and continue along the river bank.

Carry on past the last of the properties and then by salt marshes, the wall bearing right then straightening up. When it bears left and the salt marshes encroach someway inland, the path swings left.

At the trees look for a yellow waymark arrow on a single willow tree. Here you pick up and follow a path which snakes through the bushes and brambles past a single oak tree and bears left in front of the attractive lawns of a large bungalow. Pass between high hedges and come out through a gateway. Turn right and walk the few yards to reach a wide drive. Turn left and follow it. It bends right, then reaches a narrow country road on a bend. Turn left and walk along this shady metalled lane for some distance. Reach a road and turn right. Walk on about 30 yards to locate a drive on your left. Take this to Glenburn Cottage where you pass through a gap in the hedge. Continue on a path through a cultivated field to come out on Mill Road opposite the path on which you set out. Turn left and walk the short distance back to the church and village hall, your starting point.

Like many others, All Saints Church has received over-enthusiastic 19th century restoration, although its elegant early 16th century red-brick tower remains untarnished.

Waldringfield

53

THE RIVER DEBEN
Walk 12: Shottisham to Ramsholt

Start: *Take the B1083 from Melton to Bawdsey. Turn left into Shottisham village and left again on the bend by the shop. Turn right up to the church and park in the wooded area in front of the entrance.*

O.S.Maps: *Landranger 169; Pathfinder 1031.*

Distance: *11 miles.*

Refreshments: *Sorrel Horse, Shottisham; Ramsholt Arms.*

Description: *Apart from two sections of minor road walking the outward and return journey to the river are mainly on firm dry tracks. The river walk is extraordinarily varied and you make progress on a variety of surfaces ranging from riverside, sandy beach, river bank, woodland track and green lane to well-worn paths.*

LEAVE THE CHURCH ON YOUR RIGHT and set off along a narrow metalled lane down past cottages on your left. When the lane turns right go straight on and turn left along the left side of a cultivated field. Continue to the end and out through the overgrown corner via a stile into a meadow. Turn half right and head diagonally over to cross a stream by a concrete bridge. Go over the adjacent barbed wire fence and stile, turn half left and continue over the remainder of the meadow towards a red-brick cottage where you leave by a stile and footbridge into the road. Go straight over and head up the metalled drive towards Wood Hall Hotel. Pass the entrance and, at the fork immediately past the thatched Sutton Hall office buildings, bear right. When you reach the entrance to Sutton Hall itself on your right, turn left along a firm wide track.

You pass a brick house on your left and at a crossways of tracks take that going right, a green lane bordered by overhanging hedges. When you break out keep on along a grass path making for the left side of the wood ahead. At the trees pick up a track and turn left. Head between cultivated fields and at the end follow the track right. When the field on your right ends, just prior to the commencement of a line of firs, turn right with the track and head back along the top of the field. Half way back to the wood a length of hedgerow commences; just before this turn left on to another track which heads away between two further open cultivated fields. The track continues through a gap in the field boundary hedge and then descends to join a quiet country road.

Turn left, pass a pair of cottages on the left as the road bears right, and keep on for some ¾ mile before locating a footpath on the left just past an old railway goods wagon on the right now used for farming purposes. Go over the stile and follow a grassy track between fields, climbing steadily. At the end of the field go over a stile into a meadow. Head down with your first views of the Deben stretching out before you. Cross a stile at the left-hand corner and cross another into a further meadow. Leave the right-hand corner where you meet the river at Methersgate.

This is the now derelict quay of Methersgate, the landing place for the Manor of Campsea in the Middle Ages.

Turn left and set off on a five mile walk following the river down to Ramsholt. At high water some sections, particularly the first to Stonner Point, may prove difficult to negotiate along the shore; however, if you hunt for it there is a another continuous path running along the higher ground which is usually dry and easy going, has attractive wooded sections and several spectacular elevated views over the river. Look out for some delightful little beaches along the route, only accessible by boat or on foot. You arrive at one of the most enchanting, The Tips.

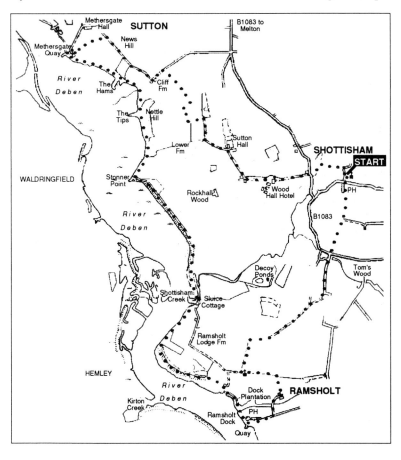

These sandy points were built out into the river during the latter part of the last century by Robert Knipe Cobbold, a Sutton farmer, in an effort to reclaim 150 acres of land. It was his intention to carry them even further out over the mud flats but Trinity House put a stop to the proceedings when it was feared that navigation and even the course of the river could be affected.

After 1½ miles of hard but rewarding walking you arrive at Stonner Point.

Stonner Point was once a manorial landing place called Woodhall Stonner where quite a large settlement formerly existed around the Green at the back of the Point. The quay here was built by Thomas Waller of Sutton Hall about 1850 for the purpose of shipping coprolite - a fossilised animal dung which was found in large quantities all over the neighbourhood and used as a fertiliser. Thousands of tons were shipped annually from the Deben-side quays to all parts of the Kingdom.

From here the going is easier and the way more defined. Across the water are the boats at Waldringfield (Walk 11). Many antediluvian shells and fossils have been found in the area of Shottisham Creek which you pass next, with beyond this on the other side of the river, the little creek at Hemley.

As you approach Ramsholt, you pass through an area of woodland before a clear well-used path develops and the last half mile to the Ramsholt Arms public house is very civilised. Leave the beach in front of the pub, once the ferry house for the crossing to Kirton, and walk up the road away from the river, passing the entrance gates and the large hotel sign. When you approach a house on the left after the car park along this tree-lined road, turn left along a sunken way through the trees. Bear right at the bottom of the valley and pass round between two properties. Bear left at the back of the houses and continue up a stony track to reach a metalled lane. Bear left on this and head towards the church.

The isolated All Saints Church stands prominently overlooking the Deben. Its round Norman tower (it is thought to be an optical illusion that it appears oval) has Saxon origins and was obviously well-suited to the task of providing a beacon to sailors and look-out post for the defence of the river in addition to its divine duties.

Turn right from the church along a firm track and when you meet another turn right again. Bear left, then continue on, ignoring the right fork passing to the left of a small wood. After about half a mile you arrive at a road on a bend by an overgrown pillbox. Turn left and at the bottom of the hill cross straight over the B1083 and head up the sandy track opposite. When this turns right, carry straight on along a grassy track which becomes a green lane, passing between high hedges to eventually come out on a metalled lane. Carry on heading down hill to the village centre and pub. Left and right will return you to the church.

The River Waveney

Listen to me -
There is a little river, fed by rills
That winds among the hills,
And turns and suns itself unceasingly,
And wanders through the cornfields wooingly,
For it has nothing else to do, but play
Along its cheery way:
Not like great rivers that in locks are bound,
On whom hard men doth heavy burdens lay,
And fret their waters into foam and spray.
This river's life is one long holiday
All the year round.

(Jean Ingelow)

THE above poem provides an accurate description of the character of the Waveney which rises near Redgrave on the Suffolk-Norfolk border, and takes a meandering and apparently irresponsible course to form the boundary between the two counties, meeting the sea at Gorleston when it appears that it should have been at Lowestoft; by taking a strange loop away from Oulton Broad to form part of the famous Norfolk & Suffolk Broads before turning east again. This loop proved inconvenient to Government planners and the land it enclosed was loped off and given to Norfolk.

The Waveney appears to have had a great attraction for the Normans, being a river of castles - five line its banks, Framlingham, Bungay, Mettingham, Wingfield and Burgh Castle (the Roman shore fort which enclosed the motte of a Norman castle).

Beccles and Bungay are the two major towns along the river, though neither were great centres of industry.

The river remains, then, what it has always been - unpretentious and in keeping with the countryside through which it flows.

The River Waveney at Bungay

THE RIVER WAVENEY
Walk 13: Tracing the Waveney from Bungay

Start:	*Take the turning off to Bungay from the roundabout on the A143 between Scole and Beccles. Head along St Mary's Street from the Market Cross and turn right to Priory Lane car park by the Co-op supermarket. There are toilets here.*
O.S.Maps:	*Landranger 156; Pathfinder 945 & 924.*
Distance:	*6½ miles.*
Refreshments:	*Pub in Earsham and several places in Bungay.*
Description:	*After negotiating the streets of Bungay, you will trespass into neighbouring Norfolk in order to follow the great horseshoe bend of the river Waveney around the town with memorable views from Bath Hills over the water meadows. A fairly long section of country road is followed by very easy walking along tracks, over water meadows and along riverside paths back to Bungay.*

FROM THE CAR PARK head back out into St Mary's Street and turn left. Cross the road, pass the church, and take the footpath through the churchyard.

The beautiful 15th century tower of St Mary's, 90 ft. high, will dominate your walk and be rarely out of sight. This was the Priory Church of the Benedictine nunnery founded by Gundreda, the wife of Roger de Glanville about 1160. It was originally both conventional and parochial and consisted of a long aisle-less 13th century chancel occupied by the nuns, with transepts and a wide-aisled nave used as a parish church. The nuns portion and the transepts are in ruins, destroyed by the great fire of 1688 which also decimated much of the town - hence the shortage of buildings of any antiquity. St Mary's has one of the most remarkable sets of churchwardens' accounts in England covering the period from 1523 to 1853.

Come out of the churchyard into Trinity Street and turn right to another church.

Holy Trinity is less spectacular but with a greater feel of antiquity. It has an 11th century round tower and Norman N window. Most of the chancel had been in ruins for nearly 200 years when it was first restored in 1754.

Passing Holburn's Garage bear left along Staithe Road. Keep bearing left passing the converted Maltings to reach the Mill and the river Waveney at Bungay Staithe.

Before the advent of the railways in the Broads in the mid 19th century, and before the Waveney became unnavigable beyond Geledeston Lock in

1934, cargoes of all kinds were transported by river and the Staithe was the heart of this historic market town. Wherries or 'black-sailed traders' came here in their hundreds, collecting and delivering coal, corn, malt and timber. Malt and ground corn were produced at the Staithe - the old Maltings and Mill still remain now converted to other uses. Wherries were also built here. 'Staithe Walks' is a short circular walk which takes you round the Staithe area. You will see a working poplar bed which is managed traditionally by annual pollarding in March for cuttings. Look out for dragonflies and damselflies along the river bank and common Broads birds like great crested grebes, swans and ducks.

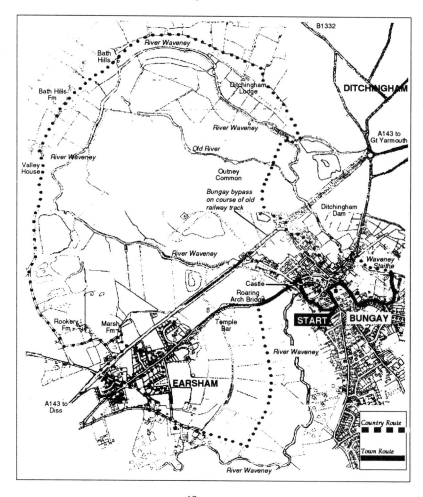

Cross the Waveney by the lock and turn left. Walk along the grass by the river with fine views of the two churches and at the end go through a gate on to the road at Bridge Street. Cross the road and turn left to take the pedestrian way over the road bridge, crossing the river again. Beyond the small car park turn right by Scorpio Secondhand Bookshop into Nethergate Street. This carries on for some way to meet Broad Street just before the roundabout. Turn right and cross both carriage-ways of the A143 to the right of the roundabout with care. The Bungay bypass follows the line of the old railway line.

On the far side head down a cul de sac and through a small wooden gate beside a larger one. Set off along part of Bigod's Way, a stony track beside a small stretch of water heading across Outney Common, but within a few yards you must leave it again by forking right along a path beside metal railings. Go over a stile by a wooden farm gate and cross the water meadows. Go over a narrow wooden footbridge to cross the Old River, followed by a a concrete culvert and stile. Continue through the meadow on a faint path bearing slightly right towards the trees ahead. Here a narrow but unusually attractive metal footbridge takes you over the Waveney into Norfolk. Although substantial, I found its narrowness and lack of a handrail on the left a little disconcerting.

Cross a smaller footbridge as a well-used path snakes through light woodland with tantalising glimpses of Halcyon Lake through the trees on your right. After only about 50 yards you take the left fork, a less well-defined path leading to a wooden kissing gate. Enter a pleasant old meadow and head straight up, crossing the drive to Ditchingham Lodge, through the trees on your left. The meadow funnels up to a group of pines rising steeply to a stile necessitating a short but very hard climb. Here you pick up The Angles Way, a long-distance footpath. The path now runs in a hollow along the crest of a steep hillside, hedged on the right but with a drop of amazing proportions (for this part of the country) on the left, which provides stunning views through the trees to the Waveney meandering through water meadows. After nearly a mile you reach a kissing gate by a bungalow and come out on a metalled lane at Bath Hills. Bear left by the sign to Coldbath House along a shady lane which descends steeply into the Waveney valley.

> You may be intrigued by the names Coldbath House and Bath Hills. During Roman and Norman times vineyards covered these south facing slopes and in 1730 a cold spring here was promoted as health-enhancing, leading to Bungay gaining a brief spell of fame as a spa town. Bath Hills Farm over on your right was the site of the original Bath House.

You pass a cottage on your right and then one on the left. Just beyond this a wooden gate leads you straight on to an earthen farm track heading through the trees. Later it continues as a grassy path. Go through a wooden gate and pass the Dutch-gabled house down on your left on a wide grassy track bordered by a wire fence on your right out on to a drive. Carry straight on along this drive, through a gateway with open views of the Waveney and its water meadows on your left. Pass Valley Farm and Valley Cottage to come out on Bath Hills Road.

Set off along what was a quiet country lane between post and rail fences. Pass The Oaks on the left to reach a major gravel works, and beyond, an old water-filled pit now creating a large attractive lake. The road is narrow with passing places from here on and busy during the week with lorries from the works, so take care. Immediately past the cottages on the right take the footpath sign left, initially along a green lane.

When it joins a metalled drive carry straight on to meet the main road via a cul de sac on your right.

Turn right and walk along the wide grass verge to the junction signposted 'Hedenham 3½ miles'. At this point you cross the main road with care and enter the blocked-off Earsham Street. Head up the street passing several interesting old houses including Dukes House, The Old Pillary and Forge Cottage.

In the centre of Earsham, which is just on the Norfolk side of the river, cross the old main road passing to the left of the war memorial and continue up the left side of the village hall. A metalled path leads you on and through a small housing estate, then on a shady path to come out between old cottages on a road.

Turn left and pass All Saints Church from which point the road continues as a wide rough track. At the ford an elevated path provides a dry alternative in periods of flood. You cross a humpback bridge over a water course at a point where it is crossed by the Bigod Way and the Angles Way but your route is straight ahead now on an earthen track, then grass. You cross a small tributary of the Waveney by a footbridge and turn left to commence a delightful walk along its right bank with the Waveney across the water meadows on your right. Straight ahead is the magnificent tower of St Mary's Church and later, as the path bends, the twin towers of Bungay Castle. You finally reach the main Earsham road at Roaring Arch Bridge and turn right to cross the Waveney and enter Bungay. Pass Castle Lane on the right and, opposite the post office, turn right into the courtyard of the White Lion. Exit in the far left-hand corner along a passageway to come out at the castle.

> Bungay Castle was built around 1164 by Earl Hugh Bigod, a member of the notorious East Anglian family which proved such a scourge to several medieval English kings. The great keep, of which little now remains, was 70 feet square and 90 feet tall with the thickest walls of any castle in England. You can still see unique evidence of undermining by Henry II's engineers in an effort to destroy the keep after Hugh Bigod's surrender in 1174 - he had to pay a fine of 1,000 marks to save its demolishion. The curtain walls (traces of which remain), twin-towered gatehouse (which you see), and the barbican bailey with hall and domestic buildings, which stood outside this gatehouse, were built around 1294 by Roger Bigod.

Turn right and follow Castle Orchard as it bears left back to Priory Lane car park.

THE RIVER WAVENEY
Walk 14: Carlton Colville, Oulton Broad & Barnby

Start:	*Take the A146 road between Beccles and Lowestoft and turn right into Chapel Lane (B1384) at Carlton Colville (signposted to Carlton Manor Transport Museum). Park just along the road in lay-by.*
O.S.Maps:	*Landranger 134 & 156; Pathfinder 925 & 946.*
Distance:	*9½ miles.*
Refreshments:	*The Crown at Carlton Colville (on A146) and The Swan at Barnby.*
Description:	*The early part of the walk introduces you to Carlton Marshes, a unique area of marshes and grazing meadows. You continue through an area known as The Broads to reach Oulton Broad, the end of The Norfolk & Suffolk Broads. Then set off on a 2½ mile walk along the bank of the River Waveney as far as Barnby. The last section returns you to Carlton Colville by way of tracks, field paths and country lanes.*

WALK BACK TO THE MAIN ROAD and cross with care. Take Marsh Lane which swings left and right and, when it bends left again to head for Turrell's Barn, you leave it to go just right of straight ahead through a wooden gate by a footpath sign to proceed through the edge of a golf course. Pass two pools before turning left on a well-worn path taking you back to the lane where you turn right. You reach a railway track, crossing via pedestrian side gates. The lane continues unmade from here unmade between trees and high hedges, and bears right to end at Carlton Marshes where you keep right along a firm, newly-laid path.

In the early 1980s many areas like Carlton Marshes were drained to grow arable crops. However as the grazing marshes are a unique landscape, rich in wildlife, this was made Britain's first Environmentally Sensitive Area in 1987 with the objective of supporting traditional farming and protecting the marshes. In winter, the grazing meadows and bleak, cold marshes provide food for wading birds like snape. Watch out for the short-eared owls and marsh harriers which swoop low over the marshes in search of prey.

The marsh drainage ditches or 'dykes' are a haven for many plants including the water soldier, which has sadly disappeared from the rivers. In summer look out for jewel-bright damselflies and dragonflies, while water scorpion and water boatman are just two of the insects which lurk in the dykes. The reedbeds contain a whole world of wildlife. Birds like reed warbler find food and nest sites and in summer there are all kinds of insects including moths and butterflies. Many wild and rare plants thrive in among the reeds and sedges too.

You pass Spratts Water and Round Water. These former peat diggings were opened up between 1980-5 and are now filled with tussock sedge and reed.

You eventually reach the Visitors Centre where you go right through a gate and left through the car park to carry on along the left side of a grazing meadow following a water drainage channel on your left.

In Roman times this was a huge estuary. Now most of the land has been drained and cultivated for arable crops, but this area covering 45 hectares has been set aside to provide a haven for wetland plants, birds and insects.

Go right and left to pass the area of Crooked Barn Restaurant, keeping along the left side of the meadow via a stile at either end. Cross the shingle drive and over another stile to continue along the left side of the next meadow. Another stile leads you along a grassy track with a high hedge on the left and then timber fencing to reach a caravan park. Turn left along a broad metalled drive between buildings and over a bridge to reach Oulton Broad with its array of colourful yachts and boats.

Across the water is Oulton, only existing as a village in its own entity since breaking from Flixton in the 14th century. It is now fast being swallowed

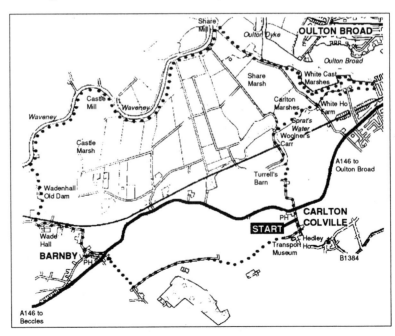

by Lowestoft which lays over to your right beyond the swing bridge which marks the end of the Norfolk & Suffolk Broads. Here the Waveney finally empties into the North Sea.

Turn left on to the raised bank and pass between enclosed hedges. White Cast Marshes commence on your right and you pick up a length of water on your right, a part of Oulton Dyke. Go over a stile and when paths fork keep ahead bearing right. When the bank ends, leave the dyke and come down on the left. Turn right to go through a metal gate to follow the Broads Walk waymarkers along a track and through two further metal gates. As the rough track swings left you leave it to carry on over the rough grass towards a footpath sign by a stile. Go over the stile to pick up a stony track by a cultivated field. When the track swings right carry straight on along the left side of a second field with a drainage channel on your left to reach the river bank. Climb it to meet the Waveney and turn left to follow it for the next 2½ miles. You eventually arrive at a sluice by Castle Marshes, a Suffolk Wildlife Trust Nature Reserve.

> There are many habitats typical of Broadland - grazing marshes, fen and clean dykes full of water plants. These habitats support a wide range of wildlife, some of which is rare in Britain. At 1½ miles you pass Castle Mill, an old abandoned steam pump house used to drain the marshes and still with its machinery intact.

Finally you come to the end of Castle Marshes and the river section of your walk. Follow a path which leaves the bank on your left and go over a stile at Six Mile Corner. Go left and right over another stile and head towards the trees along a track called Wadehall Old Dam, bordered by drainage channels. You enter the trees and enjoy a delightful woodland walk before emerging by a railway crossing. Pass through the metal gates either side - not forgetting to close each behind you - and arrive on a quiet country lane at Barnby.
Turn left and bear left to follow the lane (ignoring the footpath sign pointing right). The lane runs parallel with the railway track with Wade Hall moat on your right before turning sharp right and then bearing left. When it forks at The Green you have the option of going left to reach the main road opposite the church or carrying straight on to make a refreshment stop at The Swan and turning left along Swan Lane to reach the main road. Either way you meet the busy A146 on an S bend so cross with the utmost care to reach the church.

> The little church of St John the Baptist looks a little neglected but is not without interest. The combined nave and chancel is thatched, the latter possibly of c1300. There is also a 13th century font and two faded 15th century wall paintings, one showing the Crucifixion and the other, St Christopher.

Leave via the West tower through a metal gate and along a path parallel with the churchyard. Go over a plank footbridge and along a wide grass track bordered on the right by young conifers. Another plank bridge leads you into the cultivated field on the left where you continue along the right side, passing a pond. Another plank bridge brings you out on to a country lane on a bend where you turn left. Follow this quiet lane for some way. About 100 yards before the end of the long straight, prior to a sharp left bend, go through the opening in the field on your right. Turn half left and walk diagonally across the field, cutting off the corner to reach a footpath sign beside a plank footbridge over the ditch. Cross this and head straight over the next field on a distinct path to another footpath sign on the far side. Turn left and follow the right-hand side to the end where you go through a gap on your right and carry on as before over another field, passing under power lines. Cross over an inviting green lane and carry on over the next field and then along the left side of a field beside a high hedge to pass Carlton Grove. You enter Hedley Lane and pass Carlton Manor Transport Museum on your right - open during the summer season - to reach Chapel Lane where you turn left and walk the few yards back to your starting point.

The River Ore

Looking across to Orfordness (Walk 15)

THE RIVER ORE
Walk 15: Orford & Havergate Island

Start:	*Take the B1084 from Melton or the B1078 from the Wickham Market bypass on the A12 and park in the Market Place at Orford.*
O.S.Maps:	*Landranger 156 & 169; Pathfinder 1009.*
Distance:	*6½ miles.*
Refreshments:	*Pubs, restaurants and tea rooms in Orford.*
Description:	*This is a straightforward walk round Orford using the path from the castle to the area of Richmond Farm on the outward and return journey. You take field paths and a track skirting Broom Covert to Millford Cottages, then a country road to Raydon Hall, pass the edge of Town Marshes to reach the river bank and from Orford Quay walk beside the River Ore past Havergate Island and its bird sanctuary.*

SET OFF TOWARDS ORFORD CASTLE passing the Crown & Castle Hotel on your left. Keep to the left of the cannons and walk along a well-worn path over the grass, passing the castle which we shall have the chance to visit later.

Carry straight on, later passing a footpath sign to Gedgrave Village. When you meet a shingle drive, cross it heading for the wooden door. Turn right and left to skirt the garden of a bungalow and head away across open fields. Continue on through the next two fields. Towards the end of the last field look for a path running beside the hedge on your left which takes you to the end and down steps to a farm track. (You will take this route back to the castle at the end of the walk.) Turn right and head away on the track towards Broom Covert where the track swings right and you follow it, keeping the trees on your left. When the wood ends, carry on. You pass the entrance to Newton Farm on your left and then a crossways of tracks by the lodge gates to Sudbourne Hall. Keep straight ahead to eventually reach the B1084.

Cross over to continue, not along the footpath, but along the metalled Mill Broadway passing between open fields. Go straight over the crossroads and carry on along Bullockshed Lane. At Raydon Bungalow the lane goes right but you continue on ahead towards Raydon Hall. Just before you reach the farm buildings go over a stile on your right by a footpath sign into a meadow.

Go diagonally across passing to the right of a telegraph pole. On the far side go over another stile and walk along a narrow wooded path bordered on the right by the grounds of a large house with an ivy-clad wire fence on your left. Come out into a cultivated field and head diagonally across passing to the left of a telegraph pole. Walk over the rough grass beyond and climb a stile into the garden of a cottage. Go right, through the gate and out into the lane by a T-junction.

Turn left and walk for a short distance to pick up a footpath sign sending you left

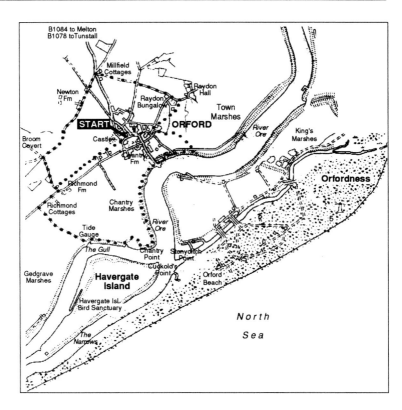

opposite the impressive boundary wall of a large house. Go down a wide grassy track and through a single metal gate beside a double. Carry on by the edge of Town Marshes and when the track ends, turn half right to continue on a well-used path known as Doctor's Drift through a cultivated field; this can be very sticky at certain times.

The term 'drift' refers to an old sheep or cattle drive, and probably comes from a time when this was grazing land, before the marshes were drained for arable farming.

Climb the steps to mount the river wall and obtain your first view of the river Ore.

Beyond the river at Orfordness - where you can see a red and white lighthouse - is the Ministry of Defence site where a team of scientists led by Sir Robert Watson-Watt carried out the early experiments in radar which were to prove vital in the early years of World War II. The strange pagoda-like structures are remnants of nuclear research laboratories.

Turn right and continue along the wall on a grassy path. You go over a stile and pass along a narrow path before opening out to the grassy river wall again. Pass boats and yachts, and a large pond down on your right to reach the Quay at Orford. Turn right and take a short detour up Quay Street as far as the Broad Street - Daphne Road crossing before returning back down to the Quay.

Situated on the coast in medieval times when the sea reached right up to Daphne Road and numerous warehouses lined the creek, Orford was a busy, prosperous seaport trading in fish and wool, and a borough sending two members to Parliament. It boasted three churches, a house of Austin Friars, founded in 1295 (ruins of the original building and the Friary walls are still visible just left along Broad Street) and two hospitals. By the end of the 16th century, however, the shingle spit of Orfordness had extended southwards to such an extent that it blocked the entrance to Orford harbour. By the winter of 1722 Defoe was writing that 'the town is now decayed. The sea throws up more land so that it is a seaport no longer'. Trade decreased and the town went into decline losing its borough status in 1883. It now comprises little more than a picturesque village with only its great church and formidable castle keep to remind us of its former importance.

On your return, turn right and locate a path following the river edge which bears right taking you back to the river bank, which you climb to carry on.

You pass the remains of oyster beds which can still be seen at low tide. Oysters have been cultivated on the river for centuries, although the variety eaten from Butley Creek today are not the 'wild' Orford oyster, but stock originally from the Pacific.

Chantry Marshes are now down on your right as you set off on a bracing walk along the river wall towards Chantry Point and Havergate Island, ignoring the first footpath which leaves the bank and goes off over a footbridge. As you round the Point, Havergate can be seen across the water.

Havergate Island, which is 2 miles long and covers 260 acres, was once extra-parochial. It has been a bird sanctuary since its purchase in 1950 by the Royal Society for the Protection of Birds. Avocets have returned here to breed and little terns can be seen diving for sand eels. In summer a rich assortment of birdlife feed and breed here along the river; in winter redshank, godwit and dunlin are among the species feeding on the salt-marsh, while warblers, reed buntings and yellow wagtails inhabit the marshes. In summer you can visit the island by prior arrangement with the warden.

The wall sweeps right and left. Shortly after this a footpath sign directs you down the bank and across to a stile beside a metal gate. From here head along Chantry Drift, a wide firm track bordered by reed beds. Chantry Marshes are to your right and Gedgrave Marshes to the left. You reach the road and turn right. After a short distance, turn left along a stony track passing by an open barn. Locate the steps in the bank on the right that you descended on your outward journey and retrace your steps back across the three open fields to the castle which is straight ahead of you.

Although only the keep survives of Orford's great castle - the curtain walls having long since fallen into disrepair and their material removed and incorporated in much of the town building - it is what remains which makes the monument unique. Built around 1165 by Henry II, it was the first royal castle of his reign, intended to curb the activities of Suffolk's notorious baron Hugh Bigod. The polygonal-shaped keep was revolutionary for that time and designed to improve defence by reducing blind corners and stopping the practice of undermining. The keep, which was never tested in serious combat, remains perfectly preserved, a monument to the workmanship of the period. The castle is open to the public.

Carry on back to the Market Place and your starting point.

St Bartholomew's Church, begun in 1166, appears never to have been completed to its original grand plan. Nave, aisles and the west tower are 14th century and there are eleven brasses covering the period 1480 to 1631. The first performances of two of Benjamin Britten's most famous works - *Curlew River* and *Noye's Fuddle.* were staged here.

The Quay, Orford

THE RIVER KENNETT
Walk 16: Gazeley, Dalham and Moulton

Start:	*Take the slip road to Newmarket off the A14 Bury St Edmunds to Cambridge road and then the first left signposted 'Gazeley 2 miles'. In the village park in front of the church.*
O.S.Maps:	*Landranger 154; Pathfinder 983.*
Distance:	*6½ miles.*
Refreshments:	*There is a pub providing food in each of the villages visited.*
Description:	*A rich and varied walk by river bank, open track, through woodland and along a short length of country road. It also includes a stunning and memorable climb from Moulton with breathtaking views.*

SET OFF BY TURNING LEFT at the crossroads, taking the road to Higham. After a short distance look for a footpath sign by the entrance to Tithe Close which sends you diagonally over the grass in front of modern houses. Follow the yellow waymark right and then go between numbers 25 and 26 along a metalled path enclosed by high brick walls. At the end turn left and cross a small meadow and then continue between open fields on a grassy, well-trodden path following the 'Circular Walk' route. You then have a ditch and hedge on your right with fine views across the valley to your left.

At the end of the field go over a footbridge and then turn left to walk along the edge of the inviting Bluebutton Wood. You then pass Blocksey Wood and at the end, follow the boundary right as directed by the 'Circular Walk' arrows. Pass a short length of cultivated field and a solitary oak before walking along the edge of Brick Kiln Wood. Carry on following the boundary left and right before finally reaching a narrow metalled lane. Turn right and head down the hill to reach the church and Dalham Hall.

St Mary's is mainly 14th century. Its tower once supported a spire, blown down in 1658. An inscription on the west side reads 'Deo triuni sacrum', while a rather patronising translation 'Keep my Sabbaths' is provided for the benefit of the villagers who faced the southern side. The church contains wall paintings and 16th and 17th century monuments; one to Sir Martin Stuteville who 'saw the new world with Francis Drake'. Dalham Hall, built by Simon Patrick, Bishop of Ely, in 1704, once belonged to another great adventurer, Cecil Rhodes, who gave his name to Rhodesia; sadly he died before he could take up residence in this delightful location.

Take the footpath opposite the church entrance running down through an avenue of majestic chestnut trees. At the road turn left and walk through the lovely village

of Dalham with its many thatched cottages, passing Maltings Farm entrance with its unusual conical malt kiln. Cross the white footbridge over the River Kennett and turn right to follow its southern bank along a wide grassy path.
Eventually you reach Catford Bridge through the trees and turn right along the road to cross it. Immediately opposite impressive entrance gates turn left along the bridleway, a firm wide track which follows the northern bank. The Kennett now takes a more meandering course, sometimes beside you but often running parallel but at a distance.
When the track ends you continue on a wide grassy path along the left side of a cultivated field. The great bulk of Moulton Church appears ahead. The path now runs through the trees and the river snakes through a deep ravine, here at its most impressive. You come out of the trees and reach the church, but continue on past as you will have the chance to visit later. The Kennett, now brimming over, proceeds sedately into the village. Cross a footbridge to continue along the left side on a well-worn path. You pass a medieval flint footbridge, a smaller edition of the packhorse bridge you eventually reach at the road junction and of similar date.

> Moulton's rare 15th century packhorse bridge with its four pointed arches stands in isolation, now bypassed for its own preservation. Being very narrow, the low parapets allowed goods being carried on packhorses to swing clear while crossing.

Enjoy the experience of crossing the bridge before continuing right along Gazeley

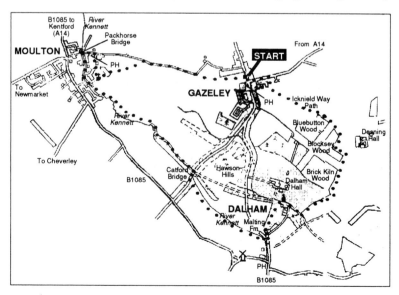

Road. At the pumping station turn right and walk along a concrete 'private road'. Go through a single metal gate and carry on past properties and along a fenced-off path beside a field to reach the church.

St Peter's Church is imposing but heavily restored. It has a cruciform plan, an early 14th century tower and Norman origins.

Your route is now left climbing steeply up through the trees to reach open cultivated fields. The exit from the Kennett valley is both strenuous and spectacular. The chalkland rises dramatically for this part of the world enabling you to enjoy wonderful views. You cross the first cultivated field and look back to appreciate the extent of your climb - and they call East Anglia flat! Cross diagonally over the next field along a well-used path to reach the road.

Turn right along this quiet country road and, later, at a point where it turns sharp left, carry straight on along a path bordered by a hedge on the left. It is then hedged both sides passing between the paddocks of Gazeley Stud. You eventually arrive at the church via the churchyard. The path leads to the road where you turn right back to the starting point.

All Saints is mainly 13th century with a tower rebuilt in 1884. There is some most unusual tracery in the 3-light East window and old glass in the windows of the clerestory.

Malt Kiln, Dalham

The River Alde

With ceaseless motion comes and goes the tide
Flowing, it fills the channel vast and wide;
Then back to sea, with strong majestic sweep
It rolls, in ebb yet terrible and deep;
Here Samphire-banks and Salt-wort bound the flood
There stakes and sea-weeds withering on the mud;
And higher up, a ridge of all things base,
Which some strong tide has roll'd upon the place.

(George Crabbe)

Snape Maltings

75

Iken Church - River Alde

THE RIVER ALDE
Walk 17: Snape to Iken

Start: *Take the A1094 Aldebugh turning off the A12 between Wickham Market and Saxmundham. Turn off right to Snape Maltings. Park on the car park at the Maltings.*

O.S.Maps: *Landranger 156; Pathfinder 1008 & 1009.*

Distance: *7½ miles.*

Refreshments: *Pub and tea room at Snape Maltings and The Compasses at Iken.*

Description: *Unfortunately the walk commences with rather a long stetch of road walking, although there are pleasant views of the Alde meandering through water meadows. The section through Tunstall Forest, which follows, has ironically been made more pleasurable as a result of the 1987 hurricane which descimated a large area of dark and rather depressing pine forest leaving open heathland. Sandy tracks follow and another short road walk before following the Alde back to Snape.*

LEAVE THE CAR PARK and set off left along the road. Bear right at the fork and right again at the next fork by Dunningworth Hall. Now there are pleasant views of the Alde and its water meadows down below you on the right.

A little way beyond the Blaxhall village sign, and just under a mile from the Maltings, you reach a country lane turning off right. Opposite, take a footpath which leaves the road and sets off along a shady sunken way. You reach a large depression which appears to be used for moto-cross training. Skirt it to the right and when you are back in line with your route continue on ahead picking up a path running to the right of a track bordered by a wire fence. Your path heads through gorse and heather gradually bearing right, away from the track. You meet another from the right and bear left to join it and reach the road at Blaxhall Common.

This region is known as the Suffolk Sandlings, remnants of a wide belt of heathland that used to stretch north and south just inland of the Suffolk Coast between Lowestoft and Ipswich. A combination of sandy soil, the dry East Anglian climate and centuries of grazing by sheep and rabbits has produced these heathland habitats.

During the present century, four-fifths of this heathland has been ploughed up, planted with commercial forest, or built on. Designated an Area of Outstanding Natural Beauty in 1969, what remains has been carefully protected and managed.

Since records began, the villagers of Blaxhall have enjoyed the right to graze their animals on this Common and take gorse and turf for fuel, so when the Forestry Commision started planting the surrounding area with conifers in the 1930s, the Common was spared.

The most ancient feature is an Iron Age burial mound 10 minutes walk NW, while to the south of the road part of the Common is scarred with large trenches dug to prevent gliders landing during World War II.

Many rare species of wildlife depend on the Common which is protected as a Site of Special Scientific Interest and is managed by the Suffolk Wildlife Trust. If you are very lucky you may even see an adder, Britain's only true native snake. Adults are usually about 2 feet (60cm) long and vary in colour from brown to yellow or grey. All have a dark zig-zag line along the back. While their bite is poisonous they are nervous creatures and are only likely to attack if threatened - or stood on!

Cross the road and head on along a grassy track. Other tracks veer off or cross your path - including a wide stony track - but you continue on ahead always bearing gradually left through what remains in this area of Tunstall Forest.

In the early hours of October 16th 1987 a hurricane hit Suffolk, the worst storm on record. Over three million trees were lost or damaged in the south-east and the conifer forests of Tunstall decimated. You will see that new trees have been planted, but the Forestry Commission's loss has been the walkers' and naturists' gain. Fir trees do not make the most attractive

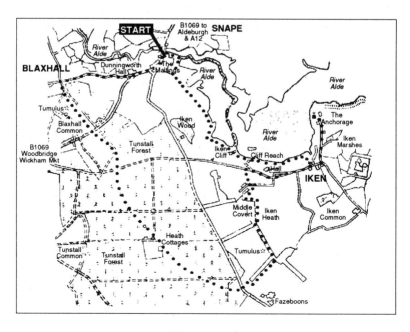

woodland walks, so what was once a dark and rather depressing journey now becomes a bright breezy walk through open heathland accompanied by wildlife and an increasing variety of flora.

You cross a track and pass to the right of Heath Cottages. What a nightmare it must have been for those living here at the time with trees falling around them! Later you meet the Suffolk Coast & Heath Path and follow it right and then left to reach the road. Cross straight over and take the path opposite which develops into a wide grassy track bearing right and left and climbing steadily. Meet another track at the end of the field and turn left along it. You pass the site of a tumulus on your left. At the end of this field go right and left skirting Middle Covert, a small wood of silver birches. In the distance half right is the dome of Sizewell B power station and ahead the river Alde. Follow the edge of the trees left and then right to head down the field, passing a reservoir on your left which attracts a number of ducks and wildfowl and passing to the left of an open straw barn to reach a concrete farm track. Turn left towards the farm buildings and go over a stile in the fence on the right. Head up the meadow parallel with the track over on your left to a stile in the top left-hand corner boundary fence where you meet a country road.
Turn right. Pass Iken Hall and the turning to Sandy Lane. When you reach a footpath sign just prior to Peach Cottage stating 'River ¼, Snape 2¼' you have a choice. Your route now is left along this well-worn path but if you have the energy you may wish to carry on and visit the church.
If you do, continue along the road and turn left on to a metalled drive at a point where the road bends right. You pass an impressive property called The Anchorage and arrive at the church.

Sited overlooking the Alde in lonely isolation, it is not difficult to imagine the monastery which St Botolph is believed to have founded here in the 7th century, possibly on the same site as the little church dedicated to him. There has been much restoration to the old building. The chancel which had been in ruins for a long time was rebuilt in 1862 and the thatched nave of c1300 has been restored following a fire in 1968. The fine 14th century font remains and the tower contains four medieval bells. Once there was a natural ford across the river here, popular with local poachers.

Return to Peach Cottage and take the path to the river bank. Turn left here to follow it back to Snape, at first along a grass path then through a sandy beach.

The area provides a marvellous refuge for wildlife. The estuary is governed by tides which bring salt water up from the sea to mix with fresh river water. The reeds and salt marsh plants thrive in the brackish water. The collapse of the river wall over the years has allowed a large area of old pasture to be flooded, extending the reed beds and mudflats

79

to the benefit of wildlife. The reed beds provide food and cover for small birds; reed buntings are present all year feeding on the seeds of marsh plants. The reed warbler is a shy summer visitor, the female suspending her nest precariously between the reed stems. The mudflats teem with small creatures and provide rich pickings for the birds. While winter brings huge flocks to visit the Suffolk estuaries, there are birds to see in any season; avocet, oystercatchers, sheldrak - which sifts food off the surface of the mud, and redshank, which probes deep under the surface.

Many salt water plants grow in the area. Marsh sowthistle, sea aster and sea arrow grass - which store fresh water in their fleshy leaves, and sea purslane, with air-filled leaf scales which resist the drying effect of the salt water.

You pass cottages along the way taking the right fork on a newly-laid path which leads to a camping meadow before returning you to the river. Over the marshy sections the path is carried by duck boards, bordered by reed grasses interspersed with the sculptured outline of tortured dead trees. Later you pass between open cultivated fields on a wide track. When this ends do not carry straight on to the road as directed by the footpath sign, but turn right along a path which returns you to the Maltings past the famous concert hall to your starting point.

Snape Maltings was in its industrial heyday at the turn of the century. Newson Garrett had bought a corn and coal merchants here in 1840 and began a maltings business. Local barley was stored in granaries until the winter malting season, then soaked in water and spread out on floors to germinate. After turning daily for five days the grain was transferred to the malt kilns for drying and storing. Malt was dispatched by barge to the breweries in Norwich, London and the Continent. In 1859 the railways came to Snape and a network of rail tracks served all the buildings.

Descendants of Newson Garrett, who had 10 children including Elizabeth Garrett Anderson, the first woman doctor in England, managed the maltings until the 1960s when the old labour-intensive methods became uneconomic. In 1965 it was bought by George Gooderam Investments Ltd who converted the redundant granaries, workshops and malthouses.

Today the railway has gone, the sailing craft visit for pleasure and the buildings have taken on a new lease of life. Visitors can enjoy a concert in the world famous concert hall, take a trip down the river Alde, participate in an activity holiday or browse around the gift shops and galleries.

In its inspirational setting, the Concert Hall was the brainchild of local composer Benjamin Britten. It was opened by the Queen in 1967 and although gutted by fire in 1969, rebuilt and reopened within a year. The adjacent Britten-Pears Music School for promising young musicians was opened by the Queen Mother in 1979.

The River Blyth

The bolder charms of savage scenery may,
Auspiciously beheld, demand delight;
Enforcing admiration, and delay,
Thy softer charms more willingly invite;
But though the former fill the roving sight
With mute astonishment; yet soon it grows
sated with wonder, and, bewildered quite,
Longs for some scene on which it may repose,
Such scenes as thy sweet Banks so lavishly desclose

(Bernard Barton)

THE RIVER BLYTH
Walk 18: Wenhaston, Halesworth & Blyford

Start:	*Take the B1123 Southwold road from Halesworth and turn right at Blyford church towards Wenhaston. Alternatively, take the turning to Wenhaston from the A12 just south of Blythburgh. Park on the village hall car park opposite the church.*
O.S.Maps:	*Landranger 156; Pathfinder 965 & 966.*
Distance:	*7 miles.*
Refreshments:	*Pubs in Wenhaston and Blyford. Pubs and restaurants in Halesworth.*
Description:	*There was a hint of the pioneering spirit I had experienced while preparing the original book back in 1985 throughout sections of this walk. Well-used paths from Wenhaston are followed by meadow and field walking with few directions and a lengthy road walk, but finally the long, and no doubt ancient, Swan Lane takes you, despite development all around, straight as an arrow right into the centre of Halesworth . Your return follows the course of the Blyth with adequate stiles and bridges but, often disconcertingly, few signs that others have walked this way before you.*

COME OUT OF THE CAR PARK and cross the road to head up Church Lane, passing the church which we shall visit later. You pick up a grassy path and fork right through a meadow. Cross straight over the lane and carry on along a path following the right side of a cultivated field. A grassy path beside a ditch leads past Vicarage Grove. Cross another lane and Bartholomew's Farm. After a cultivated field, look for a stile to cross on your right before continuing on in the same direction along the left side of a meadow. At the end go over a stepless stile by a pond into the next meadow. Turn half right and head diagonally over this to an opening leading into another meadow. A metal farm gate leads you out at the end of this meadow into a fourth. After a few yards go over a stile in the hedge on the right. Walk down the left side of this field along a wide track. Go over a plank bridge by a footpath sign at the end into a large cultivated field. Head straight down this field to the far right-hand corner aiming for a point to the right of a caravan and two fir trees at Mells Court Farm. Here two plank bridges and a stile leads you into the rough grass on the edge of a golf course. Turn left and follow the hedge. Ignore the footbridge leading into Wash Lane and carry on to the end where a wooden gate takes you out into a country road.

Turn left along the road passing the junction with the road to Walpole. The road climbs and as it descends again you have fine views over the water meadows of the Blyth valley. Beyond it on the horizon, is the mid-18th century postmill at Holton. Just past Red House Farm climb the elevated stile set in the bank on the right. Cross diagonally over the cultivated field to a point about two-thirds down the field

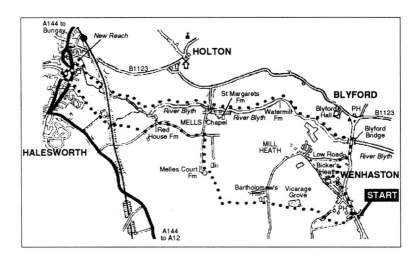

boundary hedge where a plank bridge leads you through into the next field. Cross this towards a stile just in front of the first span of the impressive railway bridge. A substantial concrete bridge with metal handrails takes you over a tributary of the river. Go through its metal gate and cross a meadow to meet Swan Lane, a path which will lead you straight on through housing estate, industrial estate, across estate roads and the Halesworth bypass (Saxon Way) right into the heart of Halesworth town centre. You arrive on London Road and turn right towards the town. Steeple End, opposite, will lead you on a stort detour to visit the church.

> The church of St Mary owes much of its size to the addition of outer aisles to the inner aisles on either side in the 1860s. Most of what remains is 15th century or modern but there are traces of its Saxon origins in the foundations of a round tower which the present tower replaced, and carved stones below the chancel piscina said to be of possible 9th century date. There are monuments, brasses or inscriptions to Henry Bedingfield, Chief Justice of Common Pleas (1687), John Everard (1476) and John Browne (1580).

Bear right - the Market Place is just off to your left - cross the road and enter the pedestrianised Thoroughfare. You leave through a passageway between shops on your right which takes you into the main car park. Walk right through the car park and leave by the steps down at the far left-hand corner to take the subway under Saxon Way beside New Reach, cut to connect the town with the river Blyth. On the far side you emerge in a small park. Walk across the grass beside the water converging on a metalled path coming from the right. Join it, but leave it again as it turns right, to go straight on heading to the left of the shelter where you pick up the river path of the Blyth itself and turn right.

You now set off on the river walk to Blyford Bridge soon leaving the confines of Halesworth. Go over a stile but do not turn immediately left over the footbridge on a path leading under the railway bridge. Instead carry on following the river and then leaving it to follow the edge of the meadow right to cross another stile. Go right and left under another span of the railway bridge and over another stile and substantial footbridge. Cross another wooden footbridge to switch to the left bank of the river. Carry on, your progress occasionally interspersed by further stiles and footbridges. At one point you need to bear sharp right towards the buildings of Red House Farm, go over a footbridge and then turn left to cut across the meadow to pick up the river again.

The River Blyth, its valleys and meadows have not always been as they appear today. There is archaeological evidence that at the beginning of the 16th century the river bed was 7 feet higher. Between 1761 and 1850 the river was very busy. It had been made navigable to Halesworth bridge with the development of New Reach and the construction of 4 locks. (The lock walls are still evident today.) Wherries sailed up and down the river or were towed by men and horses if there was no wind. They carried coal, coke and timber upsteam, grain and malt down. The round trip would take two days. In this instance the decline in the Blyth Navigation was not caused by competition from the railways (see below) but by landowning gentry who reclaimed the saltings by building embankments to keep out the tides. This led to the eventual silting up of Southwold Harbour (see Walk 22) and ruined the river trade.

You eventually pass through a canopy of bushes to reach a quiet country lane by a road bridge in the hamlet of Mells. Your way is straight on crossing the lane and continuing by the left bank of the river, but before doing so, take two small detours along the lane either side of the bridge. The first is right, over the bridge, to the collection of houses and the buildings of St Margaret's Farm. Look for the ruins of an ivy-clad chapel behind the houses in front of you.

The Norman chapel of St Margaret's was about 50 feet long and consisted of a nave and apsed chancel. It is thought to have been built by Ebrandus de Mells about 1104 and only in use until 1465. What remains recognisable is the arch between the nave and chancel and the gable wall above it.

Walk back over the bridge and carry on to the next bridge which spans not water but what was once the track of the old Southwold Railway.

The Southwold Railway is still fondly remembered by those who knew and used it. It ran from 1879 to 1929 between Southwold and Halesworth where it was intended to connect with the main line in an attempt to promote Southwold as a holiday resort. The small, open-ended coaches with balconies and tramway-type seats ran on a narrow 3 foot gauge track with a speed limit of 16mph. This, along with its many other idiosyncrasies made it uncompetitive with buses and the source of a certain amount of ridicule.

Return to the river and carry on along the left bank, the water meadows continuing on your left. The Blyth, up to this point little more than a large stream, now begins to throw back its banks and flow with a greater sense of urgency as it passes sand and graval works. Walk on through an area of light woodland and cross a fine new metal footbridge by Watermill Farm. Soon the church at Blyford appears ahead with the river continuing to grow in statute. You cross a track, stiled on either side, leading left to Blyford Hall and finally arrive at Blyford Bridge.
Turn right on the road and enter Wenhaston. Take the right turn along Low Road, and at the end of the speed limit, go left up by Bicker's End along a shady path climbing steeply. The path snakes through a wooded area with bracken and gorse known as Bicker's Heath. Ignoring paths right and left you eventually come out on a metalled lane on a bend and turn left. Head up Coles Hill to join the main street through the village. Pass the Compasses, a refreshment stop opportunity when open, and the post office and general store. Enter the churchyard to visit the church before returning to the village hall car park.

Traces of an earlier Saxon building were discovered during restoration of St Peter's 13th century chancel in 1892, but the church's greatest treasure is its wonderful 'Doom' painting which formerly filled the chancel arch above the screen. Probably painted by a monk from Blythburgh priory around 1490 it had been whitewashed over and only rediscovered after being thrown out and washed clean by rain water.

THE LITTLE OUSE
Walk 19: Brandon to Santon Downham

Start:	*Park in the free car park at the bottom of the high street beside the Cooperative Pioneer Supermarket.*
O.S.Maps:	*Landranger 144; Pathfinder 68/78 & 88/98.*
Distance:	*5½ miles.*
Refreshments:	*Plenty of pubs, cafes and restaurants in Brandon and a picnic site half-way along the walk.*
Description:	*This is a very easy walk. The first half mainly along firm tracks with a long section through woodland, and the second half following the river path.*

WALK OUT at the far end of the car park and turn right towards Leamon Court. Turn left into the unmade Gas House Drove. This runs for nearly ¾ mile partly metalled then as an earthen track. Later, when there are grazing meadows on your left you will see hundreds of worked flint and flint flake spoil scattered on the path.

Flint has played a significant part in the historic development of Brandon and Brandon Heritage Centre in George Street traces the local flint, fur and forestry industries in the area. A mile or so outside the town along the Thetford road is the site of Grimes Graves, one of the oldest industrial sites in Europe, where 4,000 years ago in Neolithic times flint was mined for tools and arrowheads. Later the industry was revived when flints were chiselled into squared-off shapes by flintknappers for building and the spare chippings made into flints for lighters and flintlock rifles giving the town a period of great importance. Worked flint used in buildings, especially in decoration on churches, is called knapping or flushwork.

Eventually you meet a cross track and turn left bordered by a post and rail fence. Pass to the right of the riding stables and by the black and yellow cross pole to enter a track through Santon Downham Camp Site and on into the woods. Later when the track swings right by a Suffolk County Council education information board you carry straight on through sections of mature and young woodland, and areas of cleared woodland.

This woodland runs along the edge, and forms part of Thetford Forest, which is the largest lowland pine forest in the country. It was mainly planted in 1922 with Scots pine, but Corsican pine, Douglas fir and, increasingly, broadleaf species are also found. Habitats are being developed to encourage typical Breckland bird species such as woodlark and

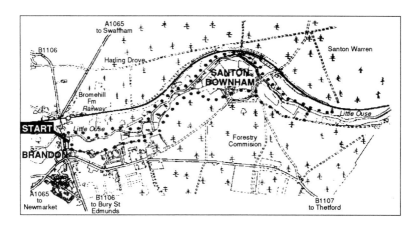

nightjar, along with butterflies such as the speckled wood and skipper. The forest is one of the few remaining places in England where the native red squirrel can still be seen.

At another black and yellow cross pole the track swings right and after crossing a track bears left. Continue now along a springy grass path through a section of young mixed woodland to reach an unmade road, passing council houses on your left and a telephone box on your right. Arrive at the road on a bend. Turn left and walk through Santon Downham along the wide grass verge with a large area of green on your right. As the bend bears right pass the junction and carry on to reach the church.

> The light soil of the area which has proved so suitable for tree growing almost led to the destruction of the village in 1688, when a violent sand-storm blew sand from Lakenheath Hills some five miles away and virtually covered it. Many homes were destroyed and the river choked and made unnavigable.
> St Mary's Church is much older than it first appears. The nave is 12th century and the chancel 13th. Older still is the priest's door in the chapel thought to be pre-Conquest.

Carry on past the Forestry Commission Woodland office and a little further on take Track 17 left also signposted 'To Thetford' and 'Little Ouse Path'. Follow this track through the forest bordered by orange marker posts. Later you pass a track going off right between two trees numbered 32 and 21. Just past this leave the named and arrowed track by turning left to follow the orange marker track bordered by a post and rail fence crossing a long impressive pedestrian footbridge carrying the track over the Little Ouse and reaching a picnic site. Your route is left to follow the river

bank of the Little Ouse back to Brandon but this may be a good place to take a break and perhaps a short detour right along the river to visit the little church of All Saints which is in Norfolk. Although no longer used it is considerately kept unlocked for visitors.

Return to the bridge and set off along the river bank. Later you cross a road beside a metal road bridge and carry on.

You eventually pass a modern wooden landing stage and go over a footbridge before following a path right, away from the river, through trees and turning left at The Maltings along Riverside Way. At the main road turn left and cross the old road bridge over the Little Ouse to enter the high street. Turn left to the car park and your starting point.

The Heritage Coast

A land that is lonelier than ruin;
A sea that is stranger than death:
Far fields that a rose never blew in,
Wan waste where the winds lack breath;
Waste endless and boundless and flowerless
But of marsh-blossoms fruitless as free:
Where earth lies exhausted, as powerless
To strive with the sea.

(Algernon Charles Swinburne
from 'By the North Sea')

Shingle Street

Crumbling Cliffs at Dunwich (Walk 20)

THE HERITAGE COAST
Walk 20: Dunwich to Eastbridge

Start:	*Take the right turn to Dunwich off the A12 just north of Yoxford. In Westleton village turn left and then right to Dunwich. Park on the official car park in the village.*
O.S.Maps:	*Landranger 156; Pathfinder 966 & 987.*
Distance:	*8 ½ miles.*
Refreshments:	*Dunwich Ship and Fish & Chip restaurant; Eastbridge Eels Foot pub.*
Description:	*This wonderfully diverse walk provides a frightening first-hand view of the effects of the North Sea on the fragile East Anglian coast. The first section gingerly follows the continually realigned coast path along the cliff top and a pleasant woodland walk through part of Dunwich Forest. You then pass through the open heathlands of Dunwich Heath. Eastbridge is reached via a quiet country road and the path then heads for the sea at Minsmere via the marshes of Minsmere Level. The return is along the beach by the crumbling cliffs back to Dunwich.*

WALK BACK out of the car park and head up away from the village for a short distance, passing one closed footpath and taking the second, a well-worn shady path to the left by a large brick house. (The footpath originally left the car park along a section of the cliff now lost). Bear right now walking parallel with the cliff along a path which is continually being moved further back as sections fall to the beach below. Bearing this in mind, it is not advisable to let your curiosity get the better of you and wander near the cliff edge. The flint wall now on your right is part of the boundary wall of Greyfriars Priory and you come to a point where you can break from the route to enter the precincts and explore what remains.

> This Franscican Priory was founded in 1277 but moved further inland in 1289. The precincts, which cover 7 acres, adjoin what is left of All Saints Churchyard - you have just passed the remaining gravestones on your left. The tower, last remnant of the church itself, fell from the cliff in 1919. Most of the precinct wall remains complete - at the time of writing - with two well preserved 14th century gateways. Of the main buildings, part of the southern range stand and consists of the southern walk of the cloister with the ruins of the refectory above.

Carry on and at the end go over steps in the corner of the priory wall - now itself on the cliff edge - where the track ends.Turn left and right to continue through a section of woodland. You reach a sunken cross-track. This is Middlegate, all that remains of one of the old roads into town. The only way now is right - left would take you over the cliff! Pass under Middleditch Bridge and soon join a wide track passing entrance gates to the impressive East Friars. Continue along the shingle drive to reach the road on a bend. Pass Little Greyfriars on the left and attractive leaded-windowed flint cottages on the right. Turn off left along the footpath to Minsmere, a tree and hedge-lined shingle drive through the woods. Just before the grounds of a large house, the drive bears right and narrows to a well-used path heading deep into the wood between post and rail fencing.

After a delightful woodland walk you eventually arrive at a country lane. Go a few paces right and cross over to continue on as before along a bridleway between hedges. At a crossways of paths, carry straight on, the bridleway sandy and bordered by bracken. Later it opens out heading through gorse and silver birch.

This is Dunwich Heath, a heathland nature reserve owned by the National Trust. With its yellow gorse in spring and purple heather in late summer it is a remnant of the wild and open countryside called the Sandlings which

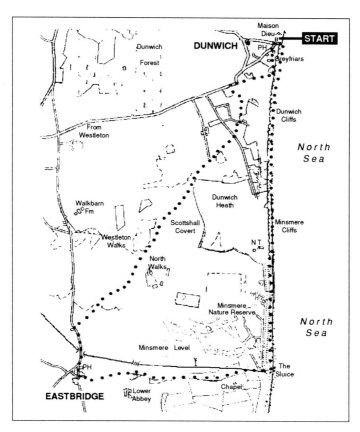

once covered this coast. The remaining areas are precious places and home to rare wildlife; there are excellent chances of seeing deer here, even a stag. The beautiful hilly scenery looks very untypical of Suffolk.

At a point where the track divides, keep to the left through the trees (the other runs parallel as a grass track). Cross a metalled lane leading to Minsmere RSPB Reserve car park and carry on as before, now along a grassy path with fields on either side climbing, at first bordered on the left by a wire fence. There are open country views across to Sizewell B nuclear power station. Eventually you reach another metalled approach road to the reserve and continue straight ahead.
The road bears left passing a property on the right. Pass over a road bridge and another before reaching the Eels Foot public house at Eastbridge.
Pass cottages and, just before the telephone box on the right, turn off left along a track signposted 'Minsmere Sluice 1½'. Follow a narrow path which runs between the water meadows, then the left side of a cultivated field. The path is then gorse-bordered and changes to a grassy path between open fields. The farm over on your right is Lower Abbey Farm, taking its name from ancient ruins you will soon see ahead. At the end of the field go over a high stile and bear right to follow the right side of a meadow with water on your right. Go over a second and third stile with a wood on your right and, following another stile, the countryside opens out as you approach the sea - this is Minsmere Level. Pass a water pump and draw level with the little ruin on the rising ground over on your right. There is no official right of way over to it but, as you can see, others appear to have worn a path to pay a visit.

This small isolated stone building, crumbling, overgrown and encumbered by having a World War II pillbox built within it, is believed to have been part of a small chapel connected with the original abbey founded for Premonstratensian Canons by Lord Chief Justice Ranulph de Glanville in 1182. The unsuitability of its island site resulted in the abbey being moved to Leiston where it was refounded by Robert Earl of Suffolk in 1363.
The surrounding lowland was first efficiently drained between 1846-50 by Garrett & Son of the Leiston Iron Works, creating the Minsmere Level. Richard Garrett III had gained prominence after producing a famous portable steam engine and threshing machine.

Walk on to reach Minsmere Sluice where you climb the sandy sea wall. Turn left and head back towards Dunwich.

On your left is Minsmere, one of the most famous nature reserves in Britain. Reedbeds and marshes were created unwittingly as a result of flooding for defence during World War II. Owned by the RSPB, it is the home of many rare plants and animals including the bittern and marsh harrier. At Minsmere Cliffs, the white coastguard cottages are under the National

Trust and it is worth a detour to visit the information/gift shop and the surrounding heather-covered heath.

If you make the detour you will need to return to this point as cliff falls have destroyed the public stairway back down to the beach further on. Carry on along the beach.

As you continue it is easy to see why the cliffs are being eroded at such an alarming rate by examining their fatal construction - a thin layer of top soil supported by bands of soft sand and shingle. Yet despite this, it is difficult to believe that, with the exception of Greyfriars and the site of Maison Dieu hospital, the whole of Dunwich, stretching some ¾ mile, now lies to your right. Beneath the waves are eight or nine churches, several monastic houses, hospitals and a town which was, during the 13th century, nearly as large as Ipswich and the premier port in Eastern England. It all really began with a storm in January 1328 which first choked the harbour, and ended with a severe gale in 1739 which saw the sea engulf almost all of what remained of the old town.

You finally arrive by the fishing boats at the car park.

The car park stands on the site of Maison Dieu, one of Dunwich's medieval hospitals; ruins of the building remained until the 18th century.
The restaurant and tea-room here has a reputation for the quality of its fresh fish. There are also public toilets here.
Along the village street is the popular Ship public house, and, further on, the little Museum recounts the history of Dunwich with models and artefacts, some from recent exploration of the sea bed. Beyond the museum is St James Church which contains the remains of the Leper Hospital Chapel - a Norman apse - and a buttress from the tower of All Saints, the last of the old medieval churches to succumb to the ravages of the North Sea.

Greyfriars Priory

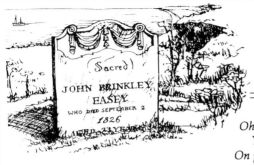

Thoughts of Old Dunwich

Oh Dunwich, jewel of Suffolk past,
Your wonders only now to see
On parchment and in stone inscribed
In some forgotten cemetery.

Thy pomp, thy pow'r O Dunwich, now's no more;
Lost is thy splendor, sunk in endless night,
Fair trade and commerce have forsook thy shore,
And all thy pristine glories vanish'd quite.

. . . For the waves care little for rank and station,
And the winds are whimpering round the dead,
Whose souls cry out at the desecration
That flung their bones on the ocean's bed.
Oh! Waste and silence and desolation -
And a passing thought for the years long fled!

Where the lone cliff uprears its rugged head,
Where frowns the ruin o'er the silent dead,
Where sweeps the billow on the lonely shore,
Where once the mighty lived, but live no more;
Where proudly frowned the convent's massy hall,
Where bards proclaimed, and warriers shared the feast,
Where ruled the baron, and where knelt the priest, -
There stood the city in its pride - 'tis gone!
Mocked at by crumbling pile, and mouldering stone,
And shapeless masses which the reckless power
of time hath hurled from ruined arch and tower!
O'er the lone spot, where shrines and pillared halls
once gorgeous shone, the clammy lizard crawls;
O'er the lone spot, where yawned the guarded fosse,
Creeps the wild bramble, and the spreading moss:
Oh! time hath bowed that lordly city's brow,
In which the mighty dwelt - where dwell they now?

THE HERITAGE COAST
Walk 21: Alderton to Shingle Street

Start:	*Take the B1083 from Melton to Bawdsey. Turn left at the right hand bend in the centre of Alderton and park in the area of Watson Way just off the main village.*
O.S.Maps:	*Landranger 169; Pathfinder 1031.*
Distance:	*6 miles.*
Refreshments:	*Alderton Swan.*
Description:	*An easy walk initially on field paths and sea wall, then along the beach at Shingle Street and returning by the river wall and a quiet country road.*

WALK BACK TOWARDS ALDERTON VILLAGE and take the track left sign-posted 'Shingle Street 2 miles'. The track passes between properties and a playing field on the left to become a well-worn path beside a hedge with a field on your right. It continues on ahead now between fields as a wide grassy path with views ahead of two Martello Towers. Go over a wooden footbridge and turn right with the stream on your right. Carry on along the left bank bearing left avoiding the concrete bridge. Keep on to pick up the sea wall which you climb and turn left. Pass by the Martello Tower on your left. The wall divides and you take the right fork slowly bearing right. At the end of the wall go right through a wooden gate along a raised path to reach a concrete drive. A Martello Tower is on your right as you head straight on passing to the right of a property to reach the beach.

This is Shingle Street, a desolate expanse of coastline with a scattering of weather-beaten buildings huddled together in defiance of the elements. The first houses were not built here until 1810, the villagers working as fishermen and river pilots. At the start of World War II Shingle Street was evacuated and the fishing boats destroyed, never to return. While much of its wartime history is surrounded in secrecy it is known that the Lifeboat Inn was blown up during a bouncing bomb experiment!

The Martello Towers took their name from Sir David Dundas following his experience in Corsica where a round tower on Point Mortella with walls 18' thick had succeeded in driving off several men-of-war. The towers along the English coast were not as substantial, having been built in rather a panic when an invasion by Napoleon seemed imminent. The South Coast was given priority, those on what was considered the less vunerable East Coast not being completed until about 1812. Each tower required some 700,000 bricks, some of which were made locally. It had an average diameter of 26' with walls 9' thick in the front and 5' at the rear; the height was about 34'. Like the pillboxes and tank defences of the two World Wars, they were never needed but stand as a reminder that fear of invasion has always been a cross succeeding generations had to bear.

Look out to sea and the end of the shingle spit. This was created when nature and gales wiped out two-thirds of nearby Aldeburgh and spread a ridge of shingle down the coast cutting off the medieval port of Orford.

Turn left and walk along the beach, leaving just past the old Coastguard Station to pick up path signposted 'Suffolk Coast & Heath Path' which bears left and swings right to run parallel with the beach as a raised sea wall.

When the wall turns away from the sea follow it and cross a stile. Continue on, with water on either side, to another stile by the road. Cross straight over and take the footpath opposite down a grassy track towards a pump house. Go over a stile and bear left along a raised bank around the edge of the meadow. The grass is short and the way well-trodden by cattle, and when confronted by bushes you will have to drop down the bank on the left to skirt them. Climb a set of high wooden steps to negotiate a wire cattle fence. The grass becomes longer and tougher but progress should be steady. Take a wide sweep to the right and then head for the Martello Tower you passed earlier. When a length of bank bears away left over a stile towards the tower, you carry straight on. You reach a point where the wall path divided on your outward journey and turn right to leave it by heading across to locate a culvert following the line of the telegraph poles. Cross the culvert and stile over the stream and head away from the sea wall across the field still following the line of telegraph poles until you meet a firm farm track. Bear right on this past twin

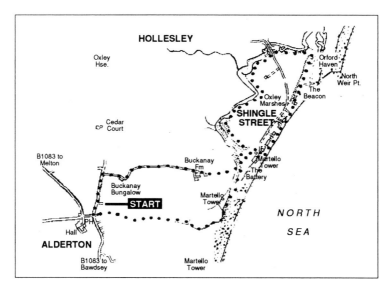

poles carrying a transformer and head for the farm buildings. Pass a pillbox and bear right and left to reach the farmyard. Continue on the track past grain silos and leave Buckanan Farm on the left as you head away on what becomes a metalled lane.

After about ¾ mile follow the S bend past a modern bungalow on your left to eventually arrive at the road by another small pillbox hidden in the hedge.

> This one was nicely positioned, it was hoped, to give those Nazi 'stormtroopers' jauntily making their way up from the beach landing at Shingle Street a rude awakening. Which side would have received the greater shock is a matter of conjecture! The structure still has its original metal doors and its round design is unusual in this part of the country.

Turn left and walk back to Alderton and Watsons Way, your starting point.

Martello Tower, Alderton

THE COAST
Walk 22: Southwold, Reydon & Covehithe

Start: *Just north of Blythburgh take the A1095 right to Reydon and Southwold off the A12. Cross the river and turn left by Pier Avenue Hotel. Go to the end and park near the Pier. Note that the car park to the left is free of charge out of season.*

O.S.Maps: *Landranger 156; Pathfinder 966 & 946.*

Distance: *10 miles.*

Refreshments: *Many places for refreshments in Southwold but none on the walk itself.*

Description: *A very straightforward walk which, although quite long, is rewarding. The final section, along the sand and shingle beach when legs are beginning to feel the strain, will no doubt sap the energy so, as there are no refreshment places along the route I would suggest a stop at Covehithe - possibly at the church - before tackling the beach walk back to Southwold. You begin by following a tributary of the Blyth; continue by track and field path to Reydon, and reach the desolate Covehithe with its majestic church ruins via Pottersbridge Marshes, now maintained by English Nature. The walk back to Southwold along the beach past crumbling cliffs highlights the ongoing problem of coastal erosion.*

WALK THROUGH THE CAR PARK passing the Southwold Model Boat Pond, which claims to have been here since c1900. Take the well-worn footpath left which heads past the water to pick up the left bank of a tributary of the river Blyth called Buss Creek, with Easton Marshes on your right (see Walk 18, page 84). At Mights Bridge cross the A1095 and switch to the right bank. Carry on by Botany Marshes to the end at a cross path.

Slightly left in the distance is a waterpump and the church at Walberswick. Immediately ahead of you is Reydon Marshes. Fishing vessels and small coastal craft originally came up to a point about half a mile away still called Reydon Quay and, according to the old local historian Gardner, there was once a bridge here called 'Wolsey's Bridge' built by the famous Cardinal who, as a boy, is said to have helped his father drive cattle from the Reydon Marshes to Ipswich.

Turn right and after a short distance meet another cross path and turn right again. At another T-junction turn left by a private fishing notice and proceed along a well-used path with a wire fence on the right, and later, as you pass new houses on the right, wooden fencing. You come out on the A1095 again via a stile and turn left along the metalled footpath.

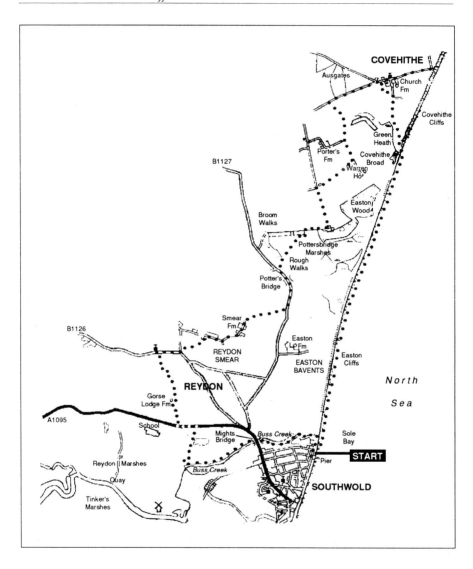

Just before the school sign on the bend, cross over and take Keen's Lane, an unmade road. Take the footpath forking right just past the entrance to Laurel Farm which follows the field edge round the garden of Gorse Lodge Farm. The well-worn path eventually leads to the road. Your route is right along the road but opposite is Reydon Church which invites a visit. Cross and go through the little white gate.

In St Margaret's churchyard you pass a large bronze monument with a winged angel sculptured by Paul Montford carrying the simple inscription "Fanny, my beloved wife".

While the church itself contains nothing of significance it is in pristine condition and invites the visitor with an airy brightness from large expansive windows, clear in the nave and coloured with late but pleasing stained glass in the chancel. There was originally a north aisle here, said to have been destroyed when the south aisle was built in the 15th century.

Walk along to the far end of the churchyard and exit by the car park. Cross the road and carry on along the footpath to the bend. Cross the road and take the lane to Reydon Smere for a few yards before turning off right along a path beside a field. After a short distance another path cuts off left to cross over the field to the far side where you meet a country lane beside Marsh Drift Cottage. Turn right and walk to the bend. Rissemere Lane East goes right but you carry on along the 'no through road' to Smear Farm. Pass between the farm buildings and the boarded-up farmhouse on your right, leaving by a rough track following the right side of a cultivated field. Smear Marshes are down beyond the field on the left and you may get glimpses of the sea ahead on the horizon. The track descends and then climbs to meet the B1127.
Cross the road and turn left. There is no verge until you reach the white post and rail fence where you cross Potters Bridge Sluice. A little further on a footpath goes right via a stile and wooden gate to enter Benacre National Nature Reserve.

Benacre (Covehithe) Nature Reserve was established by English Nature in co-operation with Sir John Gooch Bt., to protect and foster its diverse natural interest including beach dunes, heaths, broads and woodland. This variety of habitat and easterly situation combine to attract many species of birds. The broads are very different from those of Broadland, varying in depth and salinity owing to seepage of saltwater through the shingle which separates them from the sea or by overtopping on high tides.

Set off along the edge of Pottersbridge Marshes on a meandering but distinct path through the reeds. The worst areas are bridged but the going is generally sticky. You leave the area by following the Suffolk Coast Path left over a footbridge passing another information board to head up a grassy meadow with the sea clearly in view over on your right. Continue with a hedge on your left and at the crossways of tracks go right. Pass a small area of woodland and turn left following the field boundary just before a house. Continue along the track following the right side of the field and at the next junction turn right on a wide stony track by Middle Buildings, now comprising just one brick barn. With the expanse of Covehithe Broad ahead, turn left at the next T-junction. The impressive tower of Covehithe Church is now ahead as you pass a pillbox on a sandy track. Turn right at the next

crosstrack and keep in this direction along the left side of the field along a grassy path. A Suffolk Coast Path sign then sends you left over an area of green to cross a footbridge and follow a path bordered by bracken, leading you into a delightful shady way bordered by old oaks; obviously a track of ancient origin. Arrive on a quiet tree-lined country road which takes you the half-mile or so to reach the wonderful ruined church at Covehithe.

> With the exception of Dunwich there is no more striking example of the price Suffolk has paid in its continual battle with the North Sea than here at Covehithe. Nothing remains of what used to be known as North Hales except for the cathedral-like shell of St Andrew's Church, built in the 1400s, and illustrating what an important medieval port it used to be. Yet ironically it was not the sea that blighted this great monument, but the villagers themselves during Civil War riots in 1643, plus Dowsing, that great desecrator of religious houses, who "brake down 200 pictures". To allow services to be taken up again, the little thatched building within was built in 1672 using stone and timber from the mother church.

Your walk continues from the footpath you passed just before the church, but first you should continue the short distance to follow the road to its end at the cliff edge - a dramatic and memorable experience.
Return to the church and take the well-worn footpath just beyond, which goes left to follow the field boundary, and reach a farm track. Turn right on this, but when it bears left you carry straight on along a shady sunken path bordered by trees. Continue through an area known as Green Heath, keeping on ahead to reach the beach at a point just beyond Covehithe Cliffs, with Covehithe Broad on your right.

> The freshwater lagoons of Covehithe Broad and, later, Easton Broad are all that remains of the Easton River harbour. In Viking times the river was navigable several miles inland to Frostenden where remains of a possible Danish port have been recognised. Since then it has silted up. The Broads are part of the Benacre and Covehithe National Nature Reserve which stretches from Easton to Kessingland and also includes reedbed, woodland, sand dunes and shingle beach.

As you set off along the beach you can just make out the pier back at Southwold on the horizon. After The Warren, you pass a further section of cliff at Easton Wood. Here, young trees are falling to the beach long before they make maturity.

> Wind, rain and high seas continue to undermine the cliffs here which are eroding at an alarming rate - 5 metres per year is not unusual - and it is not difficult to see why the bands of soft sand which support the thin layer of top soil leave it so unstable. Earlier attempts to protect particular sections

of this vulnerable coastline have just shifted and exaggerated the problems elsewhere and so has been abandoned. Between here and Southwold the crumbling cliffs have uncovered several ancient domestic refuse pits containing Romano-British pottery.

The last section of the walk passes the cliffs at Easton Bavents where you will see one substantial house approaching the edge, its garden already being eaten away.

Easton Bavents, once a large parish, is now little more than a scatter of houses lying between the Lowestoft Road and the cliff. The church of St Nicholas now lies under the sea, falling from the cliff in the 17th century along with the chapel of St Margaret. Easton Ness, once the most easterly point in England has also gone.

On your left is Sole Bay. On 28th May 1672, a Dutch fleet of some 70 vessels under De Ruyter arrived unexpectedly while the English and French fleets, which totalled some 100 vessels, were at Southwold to water and refit. The French fleet became 'separated' from the English fleet under the Duke of York, who was left to fight a fierce battle with the Dutch during which the Earl of Sandwich was killed and his flagship, the Royal James, blown up. The result was indecisive with both sides claiming victory. The sea engagement is recorded in history as the Battle of Sole Bay.

You reach the concrete sea wall and walk up the slipway to the car park and return to the pier, your starting point.

Covehithe Church

And Suffolk! Thou has many a spot
Thus mark'd for immortality;
Which those who feel their worth, would not
Willingly, carelessly, let die;
Because the dead of days gone by
Have there done, suffer'd or enjoyed,
What lies in faithful memory
To snatch them from Oblivion's void.

Selected Bibliography

The Suffolk Garland
Orwell Estuary, the story of Ipswich River - W.G.Arnott
Suffolk Villages - Allan Jobson
Rivers of East Anglia - James Turner
Selections from the Poems of Bernard Barton
Alde Estuary - W.G.Arnott
Suffolk Estuary - W.G.Arnott
The Suffolk Stour - Ambrose J.R.Waller
East Anglia from the Sea - David & Joan Hay
The Buildings of England (Suffolk) - Nikolaus Pevsner
Suffolk - P.G.M.Dickinson
Ipswich Through the Ages - Lillian Redstone
Seagates to the Saxon Shore - Kenneth Wenham Strugnell
Suffolk - Norman Scarfe
The Kings England (Suffolk) - Arthur Mee

The Castell Walking Series

A Walkers' Guide to Suffolk *
A Walkers' Guide to Norfolk *
River & Coastal Walks in Suffolk Vol.I *
River & Coastal Walks in Suffolk Vol.II +
River & Coastal Walks in Essex *
River & Coastal Walks in Norfolk +
Historic Walks in Suffolk +
Historic Walks in Norfolk +
Historic Walks in Essex +

(* *Available 1997* + *Available 1998*)

Notes

Notes

Notes

Notes

Notes

Notes

Notes